CALISTHENICS

The True Bodyweight
Training Guide Your Body Deserves

*For Explosive Muscle Gains
And Incredible Strength*

By John Cooper

Copyright© 2016 by John Cooper - All rights reserved. Printed in the United States of America.

Copyright: No part of this publication may be reproduced without written permission from the author, except by a reviewer who may quote brief passages or reproduce illustrations in a review with appropriate credits; nor may any part of this book be reproduced, stored in a retrieval system, or transmitted in any form or by any means – electronic, mechanical, photocopying, recording, or other - without prior written permission of the copyright holder.

The trademarks are used without any consent, and the publication of the trademark is without permission or backing by the trademark owner. All trademarks and brands within this book are for clarifying purposes only and are owned by the owners themselves.

Disclaimer: The information in this book is not to be used as professional medical advice and is not meant to treat or diagnose medical problems. The information presented should be used in combination with guidance from a competent professional person.

The information in this book is true and complete to the best of our knowledge. All recommendations are made without guarantee on the part of the author. It is the sole responsibility of the reader to educate and train in the use of all or any specialized equipment that may be used or referenced in this book that could cause harm or injury to the user or applicant. The author disclaims any liability in connection with the use of this information. References are provided for informational purposes only and do not constitute endorsement of any websites or other sources. Readers should be aware that the websites listed in this book may change.

First Printing, 2016 - Printed in the United States of America

CONTENTS

Introduction	1
All You Need To Know About Exercise	3
4 Ways Your Body Adapts To Exercise	5
7 Important Mind And Body Connections	8
Nervous System Training vs. Muscular System Training	14
Getting Started With Calisthenics	19
Weight Training vs. Calisthenics	21
6 Simple Steps To A Better Start	24
5 Important Rules For Sets And Reps	27
4 Secret Motivational Techniques	30
Setting Goals For Best Results	32
7 Important Reasons To Keep A Log	34
30 Essential Exercises	39
Choosing The Best Exercise Plan For You	111
Quality vs. Quantity	112
4 Little Known Exercise Techniques	114
Maintaining Your Physique	119
Moving Up A Level	120
10 Intermediate Exercises	123
10 Advanced Exercises	161
Top Training Programs	189
Looking At Your Diet	231

3 Sample Diet Plans For All Needs	239
6 Biggest Diet Flaws	242
Weight Management Tips	244
5 Supplements To Consider	246
10 Safety Tips You Should Never Ignore	249
20 Tips Trainers Wish You Knew About Your Workout	251
19 Common Mistakes That Are Killing Your Results	255
FAQ	259
Conclusion	265
About the Author	269

INTRODUCTION

Calisthenics is the newest, most popular trend in exercise and fitness (in accordance with the annual survey conducted in 2015). It can be used to help sculpt your body, regardless of your end objective – **muscle building**, **getting fit**, or **losing weight**!

Calisthenics are a form of exercise that consist of different gross motor movements, which are mostly conducted rhythmically, usually without using equipment or apparatus. These exercises are meant to increase body strength, body fitness and flexibility through the performance of movements like bending, jumping, swinging, twisting or kicking, using only the body weight for resistance. These exercises are mostly performed alongside stretches. When performed with force and with diversity, calisthenics can yield the advantages of muscular and aerobic conditioning. Calisthenics also improve psychomotor skills such as balance, swiftness and coordination.

The word calisthenics is derived from the ancient Greek words **kalós** (καλός), meaning *"beauty"*, and **sthénos** (σθένος), which means *"strength"*. It is the process of making use of body weight and inertia qualities as a way to develop one's physical structure. Some of the most common calisthenics exercises are lunges, sit ups and crunches.

The top benefits of Calisthenics are as follows:

- You **do not need equipment**. If you have something to do pull ups on them, you are ready to go.
- It **can be done anywhere**, so you won't waste time waiting for the machines and you can save on expensive gym memberships.

- It **trains your whole body**, builds strength and increases muscle mass. For example, a simple pull up will not only work the muscles in your back, but also your arms, shoulders, lower back and abdominal muscles.
- It **supports weight loss**, helping you to drop fat.
- It's a natural, **fun workout** that you can tailor to suit yourself and avoid the injuries.

This book will cover **everything you'll need to know** to get you started with this new exercise regime; the science behind it, a set of body-weight exercises for you to try at home and even your diet. You won't find a more comprehensive book on the market, and by the time you've finished reading it, you'll be desperate to give it a try!

The military, sports teams and even schools are incorporating calisthenics in their exercise programs. It is even one of the baseline physical evaluations for the U.S. Army, which just demonstrates how much there really is to it. If all of these experts can see benefits from calisthenics, then the chances are that you will too.

ALL YOU NEED TO KNOW ABOUT EXERCISE

One of the most challenging parts of any exercise – including calisthenics – is **getting started**. People often struggle with where to go, taking the first steps and making the first positive move. However, it's one of those things that when you eventually *do* get started, you won't look back.

According to the statistics by NHS UK, it has been **proven medically that people who engage in frequent physical activity have:**

- *A 35% lower risk of coronary heart disease and stroke*
- *up to a 50% lower risk of Diabetes mellitus type 2*
- *up to a 50% lower risk of colorectal cancer*
- *up to a 20% lower risk of breast cancer*
- *a 30% lower risk of premature death*
- *up to an 83% lower risk of degenerative arthritis*
- *up to a 68% lower risk of hip fracture*
- *a 30% lower risk of falls (in older people)*
- *up to a 30% lower risk of desolation*
- *up to a 30% lower risk of mental illness.*

Now if those advantages weren't enough to convince you, how about **these surprising benefits** that you may not have known about:

- *Reduced stress and increases your relaxation levels*
- *Stimulates happy chemicals*
- *Improves self-confidence*
- *Helps you appreciate the environment – also boosting your vitamin D!*
- *Prevents the cognitive decline that comes with old age*
- *Helps alleviate anxiety*
- *Boosts your brainpower*
- *Sharpens your memory and creativity*
- *Helps control addiction*

4 Ways Your Body Adapts To Exercise

The way that your body adapts to exercise is important to know when considering which workout technique is best for you.

The body is an extraordinary working machine that can acclimatize to the stress that is applied on it. The process of acclimatization due to stress is known as the ***General Adaptation Syndrome*** (GAS). The first stage is referred to as the **alarm stage**, it is at this point where the body first reacts to stress, humans manifest a *"fight or flight"* reaction, this prepares the body for physical exercise. The succeeding stage is referred to as the **resistance stage**, this involves the body trying to adapt in order to deal with the stress. Finally, if the stress is persistent, the body's resources are consumed; this leads the body to the **exhaustion phase**.

When a stress (exercise) causes an increase in effort in the body, higher than it is naturally designed to, the body is put into a condition of overload. Overload will momentarily lower the body's capability to do work (work capacity). After the body has had enough time to recuperate from the initial stress of activity, its work capacity rises to a much higher level than the initial.

General Adaptation Syndrome

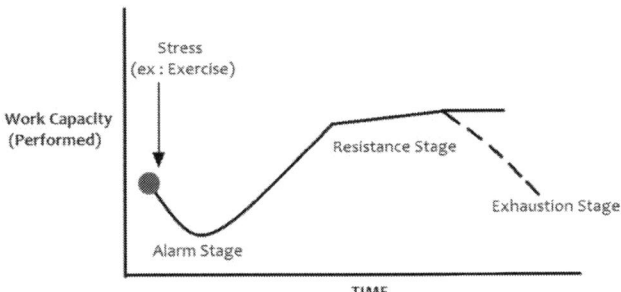

General Adaptation Syndrome Best Training

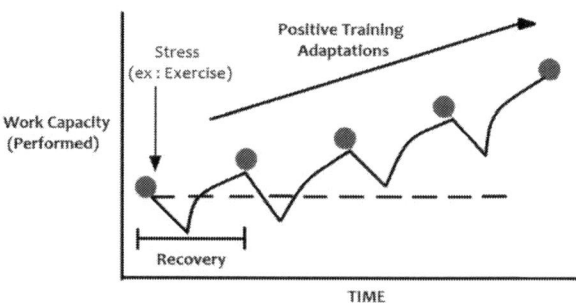

Optimum Training

There are **four main adaptations our body undergoes** when we start regular exercise:

1. Heart & Circulatory System.

All forms of training gives rise to adaptations of the heart and cardiovascular system as a whole. The single largest distinction being the **stroke volume** (the quantity of blood pumped out of the heart with every beat). This is 100 milliliters roughly in untrained people, and 60 milliliters in trained.

2. Muscles.

The muscles of a trained person have a greater potential to store fuel (carbohydrates, glycogen and fats), more enzymes that produce energy, and raised levels of myoglobin (a molecule which conveys oxygen into the mitochondria).

3. Lungs.

The harder muscles work during an exercising session, the higher the amount of oxygen they require. This implies that more air must be inhaled into the lungs, and as one becomes fitter, the lungs become more acclimatized at ventilating larger volumes of air during vigorous physical exertion, although the lungs typically will not increase any larger due to aerobic training.

4. Bones.

The key training adaptation associating to the skeletal system, involves the process of revamping which is responsible for strengthening the bones.

All of these effects are positive and promote a healthier wellbeing – something we all need to be aiming for. Calisthenics is a great way to achieve all of these effects is an easy way.

7 Important Mind And Body Connections

When considering the way our bodies are affected by exercise, it is important to look at the connection our body has to our mind.

Doctors have studied the relationship between our mental and physical health for centuries. Until the 1800s, most medical professionals trusted that emotions were connected to disease, so they counselled patients to visit spas or seaside resorts when they were unwell. Slowly emotions lost favor as other causes of illness, like bacteria or toxins, unfolded, and new treatments such as antibiotics cured illness after illness.

More recently, scientists have postulated that even behavioral malfunctions, such as autism, have a biological root. At the same time, they have been rediscovering the connections between stress and health. Nowadays, we believe that there is a strong mind-body connection through which emotional, mental, social, spiritual, and behavioral factors can directly influence our health.

With this in mind, below is a list of the **mind-body connections** that will give you pause for thought when it comes to exercise, and in particular calisthenics:

1. We All Have The Mind-Body Connection

Whether intentionally aware of it or not, each of us experiences the **mind-body link every day of our lives**. Instead of thinking of the link as something far out of reach, or something only realizable through hours of yoga and meditation, remember it is always here. Mouth-watering over a delicious-looking dessert, or nervous "butterflies" in the stomach before doing a presentation, or running a race, are all perfect examples of natural mind-body connections, which most of us have gone through at some point. Sometimes, the mind-body connection can produce negative results, like failing to meet athletic, academic, or professional objectives due to **fear originated by the mind.**

2. Our Bodies Respond To How We Think

"All that we are arises with our thoughts. With our thoughts, we make the world." – *Buddha*

This means, if we are always thinking negative, self-ruinous thoughts, our bodies will follow suit. **Emotional and mental imbalance** can start as something like stress-generated headaches, tight shoulders, and a sore upper back, and lead to unhealthy weight gain or loss, insomnia, and high blood pressure. On the other hand, we can make an intentional effort to think more positively and to develop healthy coping mechanisms for the trials and stresses in life. With time, the state of our emotional and mental health can either damage or help the body's immune system.

3. We Can Either Make Ourselves Sick Or Well

Research show that our **coping mechanisms and ways we deal with stress corresponds directly** to how we deal with severe sickness, like cancer. Long term stress affects the body adversely, and over long periods of time, chronic stress can make us more vulnerable to diseases like diabetes, hypertension, heart diseases, and some infections.

However, by utilizing our inbred body-mind link in a favorable way, by keeping our minds and bodies in shape with activity and nutrition, we can lower stress levels. In other words, the more we are able to cope by remaining tranquil and lowering psychological stress, we will as a result lower physical stress, along with the probability of developing a disease.

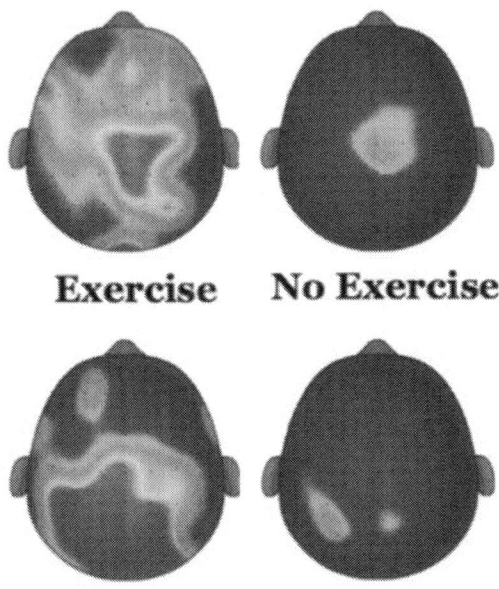

4. We Also Have A Body-Mind Connection

If we are attentive, **it is simple to notice the effect the body has on our mind-set as well**. For instance, when a lady's body prepares for menstruation, it is the hormones within the body causing all of the awful symptoms (cramps, bloating, fatigue, emotional fluctuations, etc.). Another illustration of body-mind responses is the flu. More likely, a person starts feeling absurd mentally the day or a few days before the body manifests the sore throat, nasal congestion, and other typical physical manifestations.

On the other hand, body-mind connection is inconceivably positive, be it endorphins secreted after exercise or relief from stress in the course of a massage. In the physical postures of yoga, it is thought that certain positions results to particular mental states. Backbends, for instance, are believed to activate the mind, while inversions may result to a more tranquil state. Exercise can be an easy way to boost our focus, moods, and overall health.

5. Food Affects Both Our Bodies & Minds

It goes back to the archaic saying, *"We are what we eat."* Every mouthful or liquid that goes into our mouths has some sort of consequence on our brains. Our **nutritional intake daily**, can have huge effects — both disadvantageous and advantageous – on how we feel, mostly due to the chemical serotonin. Summarily, when serotonin levels are high, we're more jovial, and when they're low, we become desolate.

Eating large quantities of carbohydrates and sugar can lower sensitivity to serotonin, which results to bad moods, and subsequently obesity. To stabilize serotonin levels, consuming protein can be the remedy, especially before carb-intake. In place of eating a sugary pick-me-up midday, go for a snack with high protein to keep the mood positive and energy up, avoiding a crash later.

6. Regular Sleep Is A Must For Mind And Body

Apart from food and exercise, **sleep also plays a huge role in keeping serotonin levels healthy**, and keeping our minds and bodies content with each other. Serotonin's main action in the body is to sedate, therefore, it is closely related to how energy is – or is not – consumed (i.e. exercise and sleep). In the absence of sleep, our brains can be adversely affected, by messing with our brain's reaction to serotonin. In other words, it is vital to keep up a steady sleeping pattern, in order to keep the mind and body fit.

7. Meditation Can Help Our Hearts

Conferring to the American Heart Association, **medical confirmation reveals a genuine mutual connection between the mind and body**. Exercises such as meditation and other relaxation techniques have revealed to change not only mind-body, but also mind-heart connections. While there is a lack of studies directly pertaining to how mind-heart interventions can aid patients with congestive heart failure, the AHA resolved that meditation could help with nervousness and depression, which often concur with severe illness.

Daily meditation for about 15 minutes can also help anyone who wants to **stay focused and calm all through the day**. An activity like meditation can help change mental perceptions and reactions to situations. By becoming conscious of tension and anxiety, and connecting to the breath, the mind will relax and the body will relax too. Even allocating a few moments out of a hectic day to breathe quietly can have comparable effects.

Basically, we are what we think, eat, drink, say and breathe. Developing and applying mindfulness to all of these characteristics of life can help us to maintain joyful mind-body relations.

Your brain health is directly associated to the exercise that you do. The neurotransmitters, chemical conveyors in your brain – such as mood-stimulating serotonin – are released during a session of exercise, but that isn't all:

If you start physical exercise, your brain identifies this as a moment of stress. As your heart pressure escalates, the brain reasons you are either fighting the enemy or fleeing from it. To safeguard yourself and your brain from stress, a protein is released called BDNF (Brain-Derived Neurotrophic Factor). This BDNF has a shielding and also reparative element to your memory neurons and acts as a reset switch. That's why we usually feel so at ease and also feel like things are clear after exercising.

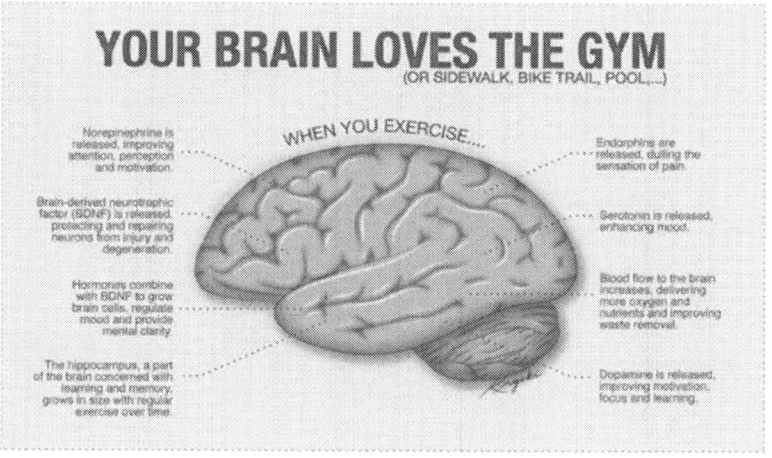

Concurrently, your **brain gives out endorphins**, another stress-associated chemical. According to researcher MK McGovern, the endorphins reduce the physical pain and uneasiness associated with exercise. They're also accountable for the feeling of ecstasy that many people testify when exercising habitually.

Scientists have been associating the advantages of physical exercise to brain health for many years, but current research has made it clear that the two aren't just merely related; rather, it is *the* relationship. The evidence shows that physical exercise helps you shape a brain that not only fights shrinkage, but increases reasoning abilities. Exercise inspires your brain to work at optimum capacity by causing your nerve cells to reproduce, strengthening their interconnections, and protecting them from damage. There are numerous mechanisms manifesting here, but some are becoming better understood than others.

The revitalizing role of BDNF is one of them. BDNF triggers brain stem cells to convert into new neurons. It also triggers numerous other chemicals that stimulates neural health.

Studies have revealed that those who had exercised during the previous month but not on the day of testing generally did better on the memory test than those who had been inactive, but did not perform nearly as well as those who had exercised that morning!

Further, **exercise provides protective effects to your brain** through:

- The production of nerve-protecting compounds

- Better development and survival of neurons
- Reduced risk of heart and blood vessel diseases
- Changing the way harmful proteins exist in your brain, which appears to retard the development of Alzheimer's disease.

As you can see from all of this study, there is no refuting the positive impact exercise has on our brains – but did you know that the first 20 minutes of exercising actually provides most of the health benefits, particularly for someone who has been really inactive?

Calisthenics and bodyweight exercises is a great way to reap all of these positives.

Nervous System Training Vs Muscular System Training

Bodybuilders use calisthenics differently than gymnasts. They are focused on muscle mass building by also increasing strength. Whilst gymnast doesn't really want huge muscles – they primarily train their nervous system.

The Nervous System

The primary thing to take into account when examining your routine is the training result on the nervous system. With the beginning trainee, their nervous systems capability to deal with intense exercise is quite limited. Consequently, it makes sense that the individual should be working on their nervous system capacity as opposed to body part training.

Nervous System Training

Therefore, what does nervous system training consist of? Well precisely with the beginner, virtually any type of training will work. This fact is one of the major reasons why there is so much misunderstanding in training modalities in the body building market. Typically, any training that you carry out at first places demands that are so much higher than your regular nervous system output, some results unavoidably occur. Unfortunately, most athletes have incorporated a great deal of bad habits in this early training, which eventually spells failure down the road. For optimum results over the short and long term the beginner and intermediate trainee should incorporate training that escalates the nervous systems capacity for training.

So What Does This Nervous Training System Include?

Nervous system training usually consists of training particular exercises through specific planes and motions with an eye on regularity, volume, and exercise choice. In other words, what are typically called multi-joint exercises will be incorporated as the basis of the training.

Multi-Joint Exercises

- Squats
- Bent over rows

- Pull-downs
- Dips
- Benches

Grouping Body Parts

When doing system training, one should exercise groups of body parts collectively to maximize the overload for a specific area. In other words, you would train body parts such as chest, shoulders and triceps on one day; back, biceps on another day, and legs on different day. There are different ways you can combine this, depending on the amount of time you have available as well as how long you wish to work out and also at how fast you wish to progress.

Frequency Of Training

Another consideration when training the nervous system is that one has to pay special attention to the frequency of training. In general, you need to keep the frequency relatively high. Implying training the body parts a minimum of twice a week. In some situations, you can go as high as three times a week; once again, depending on how much volume, how intensely a person is training, and the nutrition levels of the athlete.

Definitely, with nervous system training, one has to build up progressively. So in a very new athlete, nervous system training might include whole body training only three times per week. As a person advances and more volume can be dealt with, the body parts are typically split up.

On the three-day program, it may be full body workouts; on a four-day, it would be maybe upper body and lower body. Subsequently, you would go to maybe a five or even six-day routine for the serious athlete. This permits a significantly higher frequency and also the ability to bomb body parts over and over again with fluctuating rep ranges.

Body Part Training or Muscular System Training

The other aspect of developing a symmetrical physique to look at is individualized body part training. Size of course is not everything; particularly in the bodybuilding world. One wants to have the physique look aesthetically pleasing as well as growing large muscles.

Isolated Exercises

So in body part training, the exercise choice becomes more isolated. Generally there is more volume of sets in a body part session and the body parts are trained less regularly. To sum it up, you do more exercises, more volume in isolating specific body parts. Typically at this more developed stage, a person is considering to sculpt the physique, work on specific weak points, to balance the physique and to create a more symmetrical look. Also, this increases the separation and general out look of each of the muscle groups.

Frequency

In body part training, typically the frequency that you train a body part is much less than you would on nervous system training. So a body part might only get exercised once a week, but that one session would be exceptionally intense, overloading that muscle in every possible way and then moving on to the next body part on the next day. Normally in body part training, you would cycle more exercises through a rotation of maybe three, four or five weeks, going back and forth so that optimal improvement of every aspect of the physique is achieved.

Switching Between Nervous System and Body Part Training

In order to create balanced growth as well as size, one must switch back and forth between the nervous system training and body part training. This is done that a person can attain maximal growth as well as minimizing any impairments to the physique. There are always body parts that grow better than others and so the isolation body part training can help you to re-evaluate your weak points and overcome these inherent flaws in your physique.

In the process of doing so, we develop not only a large body but also a symmetrical body.

The question then pops up: *"How do I know when and where to alternate between nervous system training and body part training?"*

No particular rule exists on this however; one must consider it from this point; usually, the more inexperienced a trainee is, the more time needed to spend on nervous system training. Most trainees will gain from two or three years of primarily nervous system training.

For instance, a person might assign three to six months on nervous system training only and switch to a body part training for a short period, maybe 12 weeks before returning to another nervous system training routine. This should be repeated for a year or so, and then progressively performing more body part training sessions along with the nervous system training.

If your goal is to explode your muscle growth, then you should **focus mainly on Muscular system training**. Of course it's only after you've done enough of Nervous system training to gain the strength and flexibility required for bodyweight exercises.

Similarly as with Nervous system training you should pick a difficult exercise, but instead of attempting to perform it perfectly as many times as possible, you should try to perform it for as long as you can until your muscles are nearly drained. You should do **no less than 6 reps and no more than 20** (ideally around 10-12 reps). Try to push as hard as you can during your work sets, make your training sessions challenging. Your primary goal is to exhaust your muscles in order to force them to adapt and increase in size. Because the muscles can be drained very quickly, **a low number of sets is needed** (1 or 2 sets are enough). Also remember to **choose exercises** that do not require a lot of balance and coordination skills, but works on multiple muscle groups and you find them **rather difficult to perform**, e.g. pull ups, push ups, dips, bridges, squats, pistols, leg raises, handstand push ups. Most importantly, **have plenty of rest** between sets and off-days to allow the muscular cells to replenish.

GETTING STARTED WITH CALISTHENICS

Now that we've looked at the wide-ranging benefits of exercise, it's time to narrow it down to calisthenics. **Calisthenics** is defined as *gymnastic exercises aimed at developing physical health and stamina, usually executed with little or no special apparatus*. Some people find the concept of it a little overwhelming to begin with, until they research it and learn how simple it really can be.

A good demonstration of this is the beginner calisthenics exercises below:

- **Numerous pull-ups** - This training is necessary for the strengthening of your back and arms, and secondary muscles like your abs and shoulders.

- **Push-ups** - This exercise will help develop a robust chest and triceps, and secondary muscles like shoulders.

- **Squats** – Aimed at strengthening your legs.

- **Various dips** - This workout serves to strengthen your whole upper-body.

- **Ab exercises** - There are numerous body weight abdominal exercises. Having a strong core is vital for calisthenics.

These words are very familiar. The foundation of these exercises are activities that we all know – implying that **getting started isn't actually discouraging at all!**

One of the best things pertaining to calisthenics is that you don't need any apparatus to get started, even though there are **three things you should be**

mindful of before starting:

- *It takes time.* Don't expect to be transformed into a muscle machine instantaneously. Set short term goals constantly to keep you encouraged in the long run. Don't make it a short term commitment, make it a way of life!

- *Full range of motion*! It's beyond belief how many people claim that push-ups are of no use to build muscle when they can't even do them correctly. Performing all your repetitions in a skilfull way and with full range of motion, all the way down, all the way up, will make an enormous difference in whether you train to achieve a goal or just waste your time.

- *Progressive overload*: In order to get bigger and better, you need to become tougher.

Weight Training Vs Calisthenics

There is a list of pros and cons, comparing calisthenics to weight training. The two are often compared side-by-side in this way because people often favor one or the other. Of course, the choice is up to you, whichever workout suits you best will be the one to go for, but this list certainly makes for interesting reading either way:

Weights

Pros

When training with the use of weights, you are exercising your body using external resistance. The origin of this external resistance is from the weights such as the plates, dumbbells and kettlebells. One of the major advantages with this form of training is the **many isolation exercises** that you can do. Isolation exercises are workouts that lay emphasis mainly on one muscle group. We all know that our muscles are connected and they work hand in hand. Therefore, with isolation exercises, we have the aptitude to shape up or "sculpt" our body to attain our desired look - since we can emphasize on individual body parts, such as biceps or triceps etc., we can ascertain which body part needs more work.

An additional advantage from weight training is that it is **much simpler to increase the resistance** that we place on our muscles. The stronger we get, it becomes essential to raise the strain that we place on our muscles so as to continue growing stronger. With weight training, increasing resistance is just a matter of increasing the weight.

Cons

Weight training makes it so much easier to emphasize on individual body parts, so many people have a tendency to neglect body parts that they feel are "not important" or that they find challenging to train. This can give rise to **muscle unevenness**, which makes you look disproportionate and also affect you physically as you grow older.

Another shortcoming of weight training is that you need **to use external equipment**. Implying that you either have to become a member of a gym or purchase this equipment. Not everyone may have the funds for going to a gym on a regular basis or have the space at home to build their own personal "mini gym".

Calisthenics

Pros

Calisthenics consists of training with your own body weight by using natural movements such as pull ups, push-ups, squats, etc. There is no need for an external equipment. Calisthenics **focuses mainly on compound exercises**. Compound exercises are workouts that include different muscle groups working together. For example, when you do a pull up, the groups of muscles concerned are the back (mainly the *latissimus dorsi*), biceps, forearms and the core. The benefits of training with calisthenics is that you work out almost every muscle on your body, which makes you grow proportionally and attaining overall muscle strength, which is called **functional strength** - a whole body strength that can't be compared to any other type of strength.

Bodyweight training is also **easier on joints** than weight training.

Calisthenics is regarded as a high intensity workout. High intensity training places a lot of strain on your lungs and heart. In other words, you get **a good cardiovascular workout** from calisthenics too. High intensity training also burns a lot of calories, keeping you slender all year round (or as long as you are exercising).

And of course, since **no equipment is required**, you can train almost anywhere at any time.

Cons

Since you are working out with your own body weight, it is **challenging to increase the resistance** as you get stronger (even though it is not impossible as you can add weights to your body weight by either putting on a weight vest or carrying a backpack filled with weights).

It is also **difficult to separate different muscle groups** when you train with calisthenics because calisthenics chiefly consists of compound exercises. Implying that it might be more difficult or might take a lengthier time for you to shape up or mold your body to realize your desired physique.

Thus, there are advantages and disadvantages to both workouts. The style that you desire is adapted to your preferences, needs and requirements. So many athletes actually conglomerate the two exercise methods for optimal results - which is another technique you could take into account, depending on your anticipated outcome. One of the things you may not identify about calisthenics is you can get stronger in days rather than weeks, making the short term goals you set much more realizable!

6 Simple Steps To A Better Start

People who enjoy calisthenics believe that there is a fundamental science to getting started. One of the theories states that it is enough for you to train for only 12 minutes a week and here are the following **6 steps needed for preparing yourself up to win**:

Step 1: Decide How Much Time per Week You Can Truly Spend on Exercising

Be truthful. Most people shoot themselves down with too much zeal. Don't think in the realm of 12 hours, because this obviously will not work out in the long-term. Remember, you are looking for a change in your way of life. Does 2 hours a week sound more reasonable?

Step 2: Take Your Answer from Step 1 and Divide by 10

Exactly! Divide the 2 hours (120 minutes) by 10 to obtain a total of 12 minutes per week. That's it! Do not become cynical. Do not tell yourself "there is no way 12 minutes is sufficient". Simply hold on to the fact that there is *no way* that you will be incapable of squeezing 12 minutes out of your week and start from there.

Step 3: Be Willing To Exercise Very Hard That 12 Minutes Is All You Can Stand

This is where the trick lies. If this is properly done, 12 minutes will be all you can stand. The thought of lengthening this to 13 minutes will not cross your mind. In fact, within the first 90 seconds you will start thinking "how much longer till this is over?"

The exercises you should do will be discussed later on in this book as individual Exercises and Workout programs.

Step 4: Do No Other Formal Exercise for the Rest of the Week

So that's it for exercise, there can't be any more in the week. If you want to work out twice a week, that is, but this should be done in two 6 minute sessions (the exercises need to be very hard that 6 minutes is all you can contain).

In the early weeks, it is totally acceptable if you do nothing else. In fact, it is encouraged…up to a point. After 4 to 12 weeks (dependent on your starting level of training) you will develop the uncontrollable itch to do something active. When this occurs, you should thoughtfully go out and do something. It can be as physically challenging as you like, but it must *not* be formal exercise. This exercise should be practiced as play, even if others define it as functional exercise.

As you become better accustomed, the active genotype deep within your DNA will wake up and pushes you to be more and more active. Once you are at this level, keep doing your once a week workout with ever-increasing power, improving your strength and metabolic condition progressively.

Step 5: Rest, Recuperate and Repeat

You'll need to understand that the exercise you have done does not directly lead to any physical changes. Somewhat, it simply boosts your body to produce an adaptation. For your body to yield the physical change you want rest and time. Wait for at least 5-7 days before performing your workout again.

Step 6: Do Not Fail To Recall What Got You Here

By its very nature, functional exercise is of higher risk. The forces are higher and not controlled very much. The exercise that takes place is a side effect of the activity rather than its direct goal. Regardless of these realities, it is very tempting to forget what brought you here and simply switch permanently to this form of exercise. This is not the right thing to do. At this point you are actually tough and very capable to bring about forces high enough to surpass your boosted capabilities and get injured. Regardless of how good you think you are, it is always best to live to play another day. The best way to do this is to go on with a program that is fixated on conveying high intensity and low force as a way of continually improving your condition. By the continuation of a condition program once every 7-10 days, you can be certain of utmost strength and conditioning so that you can play and participate in functional movement with the highest level of performance and lessened risk of injury.

5 Important Rules For Sets And Reps

Now that you know what to do to get started, it's time to look at the sets and reps you'll want to consider. Below are 5 rules to help you out:

1. Go for low repetitions

Bodybuilders emphasize on low recurrences. Their objective is to develop size, so they overload the muscle faster, causing micro tears letting the muscle grow. If you desire to develop size using calisthenics the same thing has to be done. You can't get into a rhythmic order of movement and crank out hundreds of jumping jacks or squats in the rep ranges of 30-40. You have to drop that number. You have to carry out **rep ranges within about 8-12 for muscular hypertrophy** or **strength intensification**.

These are two methods to aid you with this rule, achieving the most out of your low reps:

Method 1: Angular Training

Angular Training is basically a technique of regulating the angle of your body to do a more difficult exercise. For instance, if you want to perform a push up which is more difficult you can place your feet on a chair. This position angles your body downward and focuses on your upper pecs. There are several ways of angling your body to render an exercise more challenging. Play around with your body angle in the course of doing calisthenics to make an exercise more challenging.

Method 2: Adjust Your Weight Distribution

Weight distribution is an exceptionally effective way of tiring the muscle fast. For instance, let's use the push up illustration again. At a guess, you have reached a particular point in your push up capacity and can crank out 40-50 in a row. That's awesome. The problem is that if you keep performing those many reps then you will not be attaining size. You'll only be exercising toward muscular strength. In place of keeping your weight distribution 50/50 on both arms shift your weight to one side so that it's about 70/30 or 80/20. Then attempt your push-ups. You'll immediately and dramatically alter the difficulty of the exercise. Keep regulating your weight while you do your push-ups so that you fatigue in the 8-12 rep range. Then switch sides.

For endurance however you should emphasize on a lot of reps.

2. Do multiple sets

Another significant difference between customary body building and calisthenics is the fact that body builders carry out more sets of the same exercise. Their objective again is to tire the muscle and tear tissue. To be able to do this you need to perform several sets of the same exercise. Most body building routines consist of at least 4 sets and more. However, more sets are required for strength training than for mass building. Alternatively, if you objective is to work on your endurance, then you should do fewer sets.

The reason why various sets are so vital for developing muscle is because **it takes *time* to completely fatigue the muscle**. You need to constantly bring the same muscle to fatigue in order to tear muscle tissue. Note that because muscles can be exhausted very quickly, therefore it might be sufficient to do only one or two sets in relation to some theories.

3. Split your workout plans

A split plan is where you train one body part a day. For instance, you do a chest workout on Monday, Back workout on Tuesday, Legs on the following day, etc.

This helps to bring your muscle to full fatigue; it will need more than one day off to recuperate. Be mindful that the muscle does not grow while you are working out. Working out tears the muscle tissue. **Growth occurs *after* the workout** when you are resting the muscle. The body is able to restore the damage over a period of a couple days and rebuilds it stronger and bigger.

4. Isolate your muscles

If you want to build muscle then you need to do more isolation and target the particular muscle. When you do your workouts allocate more time to each muscle group.

5. Progressively overload

Progressive Overload implies that **your workout gets tougher and tougher** over time. The way to make it tougher is to **intensify one of several different factors**. Here are some of them:

1. Number of exercises to be done in each session. For example, say you are carrying out a chest workout. You can tack on extra X Push Ups at the close of your workout.
2. Number of sets for each exercise. Instead of undertaking 3 sets of push-ups you could do 4, 5 or even 6 sets. Your muscles will not be familiar with it so they will fatigue faster.
3. Number of workouts per week. Pay attention to this one because you CAN over train. Regulating the number of workouts each week can be a very efficient method of gradually overloading the muscle. If you are familiar with 4 workouts per week add a 5th or 6th workout to your week.

The number of reps and sets that you chose to do is personalized to your situation and end goal. You *must* ensure that you work yourself hard enough to make a difference.

4 Secret Motivational Techniques

Now that you know how to get started with calisthenics and bodyweight exercises, it's time to look at **how to keep yourself motivated**. We will look at the specific exercises you'll be taking part in later on in this book, for now we're going to concentrate on how to keep you on the right path to success.

Economists and psychologists have been studying how to crack the code of what compels us to repeatedly do something we don't always want to do. Here are some of their **best strategies.**

1. Give Yourself a Real Reward

Unquestionably, some people may be encouraged by elusive goals such as "better health" or "weight control." But if that's not doing it for you, make the profits of working out more tangible, such as treating yourself to a smoothie or a treat later.

With time, the encouragement becomes intrinsic, as the brain starts associating sweat and pain with the gush of endorphins - those feel-good chemicals released in the brain responsible for that "I-feel-freaking-amazing" rush you get after an awesome gym session. Once you've taught your brain to recognize that the workout itself is the reward, you won't even want the treat.

2. Sign a Commitment Contract

We can make promises to ourselves all through the day, but research shows we're more likely to fulfill pledges when we make them in front of friends.

You can render the bet more credible by signing a contract approving to pay a friend $20 every time you miss a workout. Saying *"I'm going to make a pledge to do something for a definite amount of time, for instance exercising 30 minutes three times a week for 12 weeks. If I don't do it, I'm going to pay some kind of price, be it monetary or the embarrassment of having friends know I didn't live up to my word."*

3. Rethink Positive Thinking

People devoted to optimistic thinking have long promoted envisioning the benefits of a behaviour as a motivational tactic. For instance, when deciding if to get out of bed to go running in the morning, it aids you to imagine how the sun will feel on your face as you run around the reservoir. Or how delighted you'll be when you see your new muscles developing.

After ascertaining your wish and envisioning the outcome, you have to identify what's holding you back - a technique called "**mental contrasting**." In a single study of 51 female students who claimed they wanted to consume fewer junk food snacks, researchers asked each woman to visualize the benefits of eating better foods. Those who identified the trigger that made healthful snacking difficult for them - and came up with a plan to reach for fruit when cravings hit - were most fruitful at sticking to their goal.

Feel too tired to visit the gym after work? After imagining the hindrance, you can figure out what can be done to overcome it and make a plan. For example, you can switch to morning or lunchtime training or go straight to the gym instead of first stopping at home.

4. Get Paid

Still struggling? It may be time to divert to cold, hard cash. Research looking at monetary motivations and exercise found that people who were paid $100 to visit the gym doubled their rate of attendance. If you don't have a generous benefactor, check out the application called *Pact*, where a community of fellow users will literally pay you to respect your schedule.

Setting Goals For Best Results

Setting achievable targets is an amazing way to keep you on the right track.

When setting your fitness goals, you need to take into consideration **three separate targets**. The primary goal should be your **weekly goal**; this goal should include things like, the number of times you want to exercise in the week, the intensity of those workouts, and slight adjustments to your diet. When starting for the first time, you should be sure to set goals that aren't going to be very tough, it isn't possible you'll be able to jump into working out 2 hours a day, 6 days a week. During your first week, you should try for 2 or 3 days in the week, 10 to 20 minutes per day. If after the first week you notice this too easy, adjust to what you think you could deal with, but don't attempt rushing into it because you will be far more likely to fail.

Your **monthly goal** should be the second goal. This involves something connected to your exercises, something physical you'd like to accomplish, be it an increase in muscle size, or being able to do more reps, or being able to properly perform a new variation. This type of goal is your monthly goal. You might want to wait to set this goal after your first week so you'll have a better idea of what you can do, and what you should be able to do within one month. Remember to be realistic, you are not going to be able to perform pistol squats just after a month, a decent goal would be something like, being able to do 50 push-ups, or 15 pull-ups without rest. You will be surprised that, as long as you set a reachable goal, you will possibly achieve it sooner than you expected on your first month, this is usually referred to as "nooby gains", appreciate them.

Lastly, the **long-term goal**. This goal would be the determining factor for whether bodyweight training is okay for you. This goal should be thought of prior to committing to any program/routine. What is it that you want to achieve from working out? Do you just want to look good in a bathing suit and fit in a t-shirt? Or do you want to be able to go rock climbing, and do other extreme sports. Do you want to be more flexible and active than you have been before? Or do you want to be capable of lifting heavy things and compete in gym Olympics. If you just want to look good, consider some "biotastic" work outs. If you want to lift heavy things and compete in gym Olympics, then I suggest you consider a solid strength building barbell program. If your long-term objective is to break open many of the "limits" of your body that you've lead yourself to believe then bodyweight training is right for you. Once you know what type of training is best for you, you should then think, *"what do I want to be capable of doing in 6 months?"*. This will vastly differ for each person, but ask yourself what you want to be capable of doing. Unless you are very weighty, I don't think your objective should be "lose 30 pounds" or whatever of the sort. If your objective is to achieve strength, then your goal should be something like, "be able to do at least 5 reps of pistol squats", or "be able to do no less than 3 one-handed push-ups".

This will differ for everybody given their present physical condition and their personal body. You won't be able to find a universal answer of what you are capable of in 6 months. If you get a personal coach, he/she can give you a good idea of what you may be able to achieve for yourself, but that is totally up to how devoted you are, your diet, and your genetics.

7 Important Reasons To Keep A Log

Keeping a log helps keep you on track, in line with the goals you have set. It's highly recommended that you do this, no matter what exercise you take up. Writing down everything that you've done makes it more real, and is much more likely to fuel you to keep it up, than if you don't do it.

As calisthenics is a slow building exercise plan, it's good to physically see the difference that's happening within you - it'll ensure that you never want to give up!

It is likely that your initial goal will be to add on to your sets and reps on a weekly basis - even a 1% increase will make a massive difference to you and could more than double your strength in just two years. You can ensure that this is being done if you're looking at it, and seeing what's happening.

Below are **7 very good reasons why you should keep track of the workout** you're doing. These should encourage you to get to work right away:

1. It keeps you honest.

How many times have you gone to the gym or calisthenics park without a clear strategy of what you wanted to do? Did you complete your workout effectively? Or did you miss out on some exercises and sets because you simply weren't "feeling it"? Having your workout written out before time in your exercise log gets rid of the mental struggle we take part in, the back-

and-forth where we try to legitimize walking out early.

2. You'll make better goals.

The only thing worse than not setting goals is setting impractical goals. Generating go-getting goals that push you to your limits are great, but huge and ultimately unrealistic goals leading you to fall short only help to discourage and demoralize. Seeing how rapidly (or alternatively, how slowly) you advance in your workouts offers you the feedback essential to set fitness goals that are realistic, and will keep you from discouraging and demoralizing yourself too early.

3. You'll get inspired.

One of the most worthwhile aspects of keeping track of your workouts is being able to occasionally flip through and look over the work you have done. You'll realize results where you burst through plateaus, where you ran longer and faster than you ever thought possible, where you strung together 14 successive days of workouts. These achievements in your fitness past will fill you with a sense of pride and retell you just how capable you indeed are. More essentially, it will give you that reminder of fire in your belly to get back at it.

4. You'll find patterns.

Taking note of your workouts and your diet, rest and stress levels will let you find patterns for why you feel like monstrous some days, while on other days you drag your feet, barely interested in going for a walk, let alone exercising. How many times have you not felt finest in the course of your workout, and not really concerned asking yourself why? Chances are you passed it off, and marched along with your day, not bothering to consider why you felt off. Typically, the reasons aren't completely obvious; a bad night's rest, poor nutrition the day before, and so on. Having all that information can let you establish patterns so in order to maximize the days when you feel like a boss, and minimize the ones where you don't feel so wonderful. Think of it as the ultimate feedback circle for your physical health.

5. You'll exercise harder.

An aspect of possessing a workout journal that most people don't essentially think about is the need to write out a good workout each day. The thought of having to write out a bad workout can actually keep you from owning one. Rise and falls in motivation and focus will happen at the workout place, but regularly the fear of detailing a less than stellar workout will claim superiority of the yearning to bounce early.

6. You'll have a plan for your goals.

Not only can a workout log help you set better goals, it can also be the battle plan for attaining them. Whether the goals are ultra-short term (that day), or big daring long term goals, you can measure and track all of them within the leaves of an exercise log. Your log doesn't need strict set and calorie counts; it can also be a plan for your goals.

7. It'll give you a chance to vent.

Trail your fitness routine, and then write out how you felt that day, as well as your mood, any additional factors that affected your workout, or anything else that is bouncing around that brain of yours. Your workout log provides you a chance to vent, and offers a judgment-free sounding board for how you're feeling.

But **how do you go about setting out this journal?**

Tracking your workouts should accomplish *3 goals*:

1. It should be quick and easy, so that you can spend time exercising. Your time should not be spent on recording work but on doing the work.
2. It should be of use. Our current world is overflowing with data and most of it is never acted on. A better scheme is one that records the necessary information of what you have done (so you can see your development), that decreases errors while you're working out (so that you can be more effective with your time), and that will aid you in making informed decisions about what to do during your next workout.
3. It should be flexible. Even if you change your workout program, you shouldn't have to edit the way you log it.

So, with those goals in mind, here is **The System**.

CALISTHENICS

STEP 1: Write your weight and the date at the top of the page.

You can do this just before your pre-workout. Make it a part of your routine.

STEP 2: Write your planned workout program for the day in the following format:

[Exercise] – (Weight - *optional*) – [Sets] x [Reps]

Write out what you expect to do that day. This may be challenging at first, but will become easier as you become more used to your workout. This is where you need to begin adding on reps and sets as you progress. Sticking to exactly the same all the time will get you nowhere.

STEP 3: Record score marks as you complete your work sets.

When you're in the middle of a workout, it can be easy to forget what set you just completed, so it's best to tally as you go. Make this a part of your routine:

- Do the exercise.
- Make a tally mark.
- Start the stopwatch to record your rest interval.
- Change to next set.

- Repeat.

STEP 4: Vary this basic structure as required for the training session.

The beauty of this system is that it's incredibly versatile while still being clean and simple for any given workout. You can edit it to suit whatever activity you're doing:

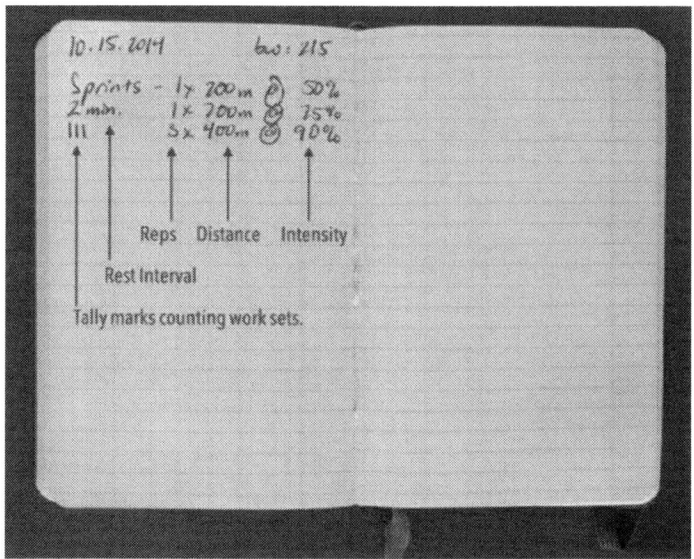

There are certainly a few athletes who are too analytical about their training. A log book can be messy with too much analysis and detail. Be careful of this! The classic saying, "Paralysis by analysis" is to be circumvented if possible! Recall the primary reason you are training and running is for enjoyment and relaxation, and of course for some results. Use the journal with these principal feelings in mind, so the journal does not get you bogged down.

30 ESSENTIAL EXERCISES

So now is the time to look at the top calisthenics exercises for you to try yourself at home.

1. Push Ups

Here is a great step-by-step guide for **doing push-ups correctly**:

When it comes to push-ups, your form is vital. Each push up needs to be done flawlessly so that your total reps measured from workout to workout are on equal footing. If you did thirty perfect push-ups two days ago, and today you did sixty push-ups by going down only halfway, sticking your ass up in the air, etc., it's totally impossible to determine if you got any stronger.

Here's how to get **set up to do a push up**:

- When on the ground, set your hands at a distance that is somewhat wider than shoulder-width apart. Depending on your forte and experience, angle your hands in a way that feels comfortable to you. Typically, your hands should be arranged so that your middle finger points straight up and away from you. You can also turn your hands slightly inwards if it's less stressful on your wrists, or you can do your push-ups on your knuckles (as long as you're on an almost soft surface like grass or carpet).

- Arrange your feet in a way that feels right and comfortable to you. For some, it might be shoulder width apart and for others, it might be that the feet are touching. In general, the wider apart your feet, the steadier you'll be for your push-ups, and will make it easier to complete.

- Regard your body as one gigantic straight line - from the top of your head down to your heels. Your butt should not be sticking way up in the air or drooping.

- If you have a problem getting the correct form with your body, try this: clamp your butt together, and then tighten your abs. Your core will be engaged, and your body should be in that straight line. If you have not been doing push-ups correctly, this might be a big alteration for you.

- Your head should be looking slightly ahead of you, not straight down. If you're doing them correctly, your chin and not your nose should be the first part of your head to touch the floor. Looking up helps you keep your body in line, but feel free to look down if that helps you concentrate more.

- At the topmost of your push up, your arms should be straight and supporting your weight. You're now ready to do a push up.

- If you are too feeble to do this strict marine push-up, do it from your knees. If you are too weak to do it from your knees, then do only the lowering part, lowering as slowly as possible.

Here's how to *complete one repetition of a push up*:

- With your butt tightened, arms straight and abs braced, gradually lower yourself until your elbows are at a 90 degree angle or lesser. Depending on your level of skill, age, and flexibility, 90 degrees might be the lowest you're able to go, but you can go down until your chest (not face), touches the floor. To make it more complex, always start the first inch very gradually, taking 3 seconds to move the first inch and then keep the smooth movement going.

- Try not to let your elbows go flying way out with each cycle. Keep them moderately close to your body, and take note of when they start to fly out when you get exhausted.

- When your chest touches the floor (or your arms go down to a 90 degree angle), pause a little and then slowly move yourself back up until you're back in the same position. To make it tougher, you can share the movement in halves. Do the first half (bottom position to elbows bent at 90 degrees) until complete exhaustion. After you have exhausted the bottom half, do the top half (elbows from 90 degrees to almost complete extension) until complete fatigue.

- Congratulations, you just performed a correct push up. Recall - ten worthy push-ups and 5 crappy ones are hard to quantify against eleven good push-ups. If you can do only ten of something, record your results and target for 11 next time. Perfect form allows you to keep track of your developments week over week.

If you would like to reduce joint strain and engage more muscles while doing a pushup, take a close look at the Perfect Push Up. This is a very simple and inexpensive piece of equipment which is a must have for bodyweight exercises.

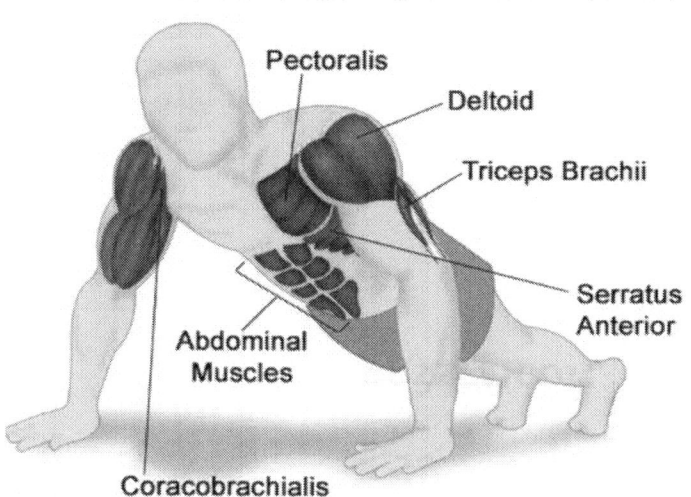

2. Pull Ups

Pull ups are one of the most challenging callisthenic exercises to do. Pull-ups and chin-ups are sometimes used interchangeably – some say they're the same and some say they're different.

The ***several forms of pull ups*** are:

- **Perpendicular pull ups** - Palms facing each other on parallel bars (bars perpendicular to the torso). Be certain to find a suitable piece of equipment that lets you do this exercise.
- **Thumb-less grip pull ups** - No thumbs in the course of doing pull ups!
- **Mixed Grip Pull ups** - Utilizing a different grip for left and right hands. For instance, left hand faces you and right hand faces away.
- **Fat Bar Pull ups** - Utilizing a "fat" bar aids gripping power and strengthens the forearm enormously.
- **Horizontal Pull ups** - Lay your body parallel to the ground, back facing the floor, by droopy from a support bar with your arms and using support equipment to support your feet - your body will be horizontal. Do pull ups with your arms while in this position.

- **Towel Pull ups -** Using a towel thrown over a support bar, you grip the ends of the towel and do the pull up.

- **Kipping Pull ups -** "Kipping" consists of a hip snap that creates additional momentum that will lift the body with slight upper body pulling. It is an effective technique for getting your chin over the bar but is not a good technique for isolating or targeting the muscles of the upper back.

- **One Arm pull up** - Exactly, one arm only pull up! This is an extremely advanced callisthenic exercise demanding incredible strength. It may not seem possible, but it has been done. Maybe you'll not be able to do this in your lifetime, but that's okay! The substitute is to grab the pull-up bar with one hand and have your other hand hold the forearm of the arm holding the pull-up bar - also called a supported or assisted one arm pull up.

Common mistakes with pull ups:

As challenging as pull ups are, do not cheat yourself out of appropriate technique and form. Some people do not complete the range of motion essential for doing a pull up and are thus do not profit from the exercise. The most common mistakes are:

- Not going all the way down and straightening the arms. Going all the way down to a "dead hang" is the correct way to do a full pull up.

- Avoid using your hips or legs to force yourself up (unless you're doing kipping pull ups). Making use of only your upper body will target the correct muscles to build strength.

- Not pulling yourself over the bar. If you're getting only your forehead or hair over the bar you are using to perform the pull up, you are dishonest to yourself! Get your entire head over the bar, or better yet, let the bar touch your chest.

- Breathing - Make sure you breathe in while going up and breathe out while going down.

Okay maybe it's just too tough to follow all the rules, bend them only if you're really having a difficulty – but keep working in the direction of proper form! Don't continue working up to 10 "half pull ups" when you really can only do 5 with proper technique.

It entails a lot of practice to level up the number of repetitions with pull ups. Remember, this is a demanding calisthenics exercise so do not feel dispirited because you cannot do more than a couple, or even none. Practice makes perfect.

If you discover yourself unable to perform a pull up, you can always get the **Iron Gym Total Upper Body Workout Bar** to practice at home.

3. Dip

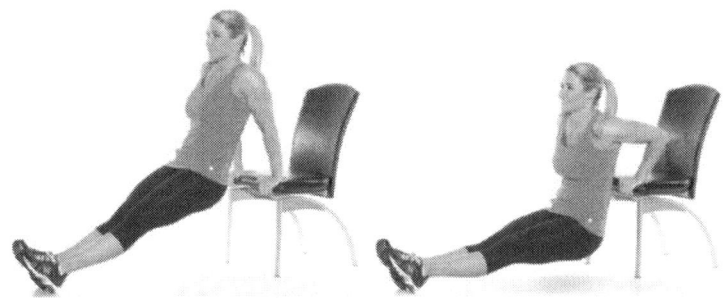

Here are the four **dips exercises used by calisthenics beginners**:

Band-assisted dips: Loop each end of a resistance band around each dip bar handle. Suppose the initial dip position, with arms extended, and put your knees against the band. Lower your body against the resistance band till your elbows are at 90 degrees. Dip up to the starting position until your elbows are straight. This dip variation makes the movement easier at the bottom, with insignificant assistance at the top.

Tip: Use weaker bands as you get sturdier to smoothly transition to full body weight dips.

Jumping dips with negatives: Grip the dip bars, with your feet on the floor (or on the dip station platform). Then jump to give your body just adequate momentum in order to complete the positive rep. Emphasize on the negative by gradually lowering yourself down.

CALISTHENICS

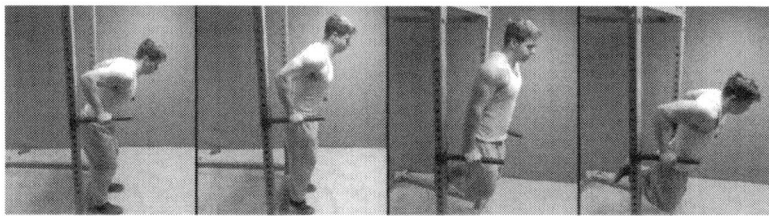

Assisted dip machine: Set the weight stack to the preferred level; the more weight utilized, the more assistance provided. Grip the handles, spread your arms and kneel on to the sliding platform. Lower your body by bending your arms until your elbows are at 90 degrees before going back to the starting position.

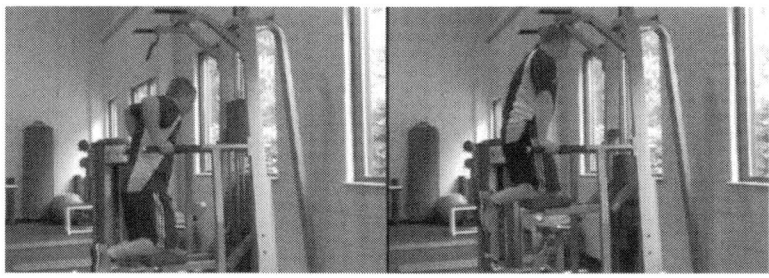

Bench dips

- Grasp the edge of the bench.
- Keep your feet together and legs straight.
- Lower your body straight down gradually and press back up forcefully.
- Keep your elbows pointing back and back straight.

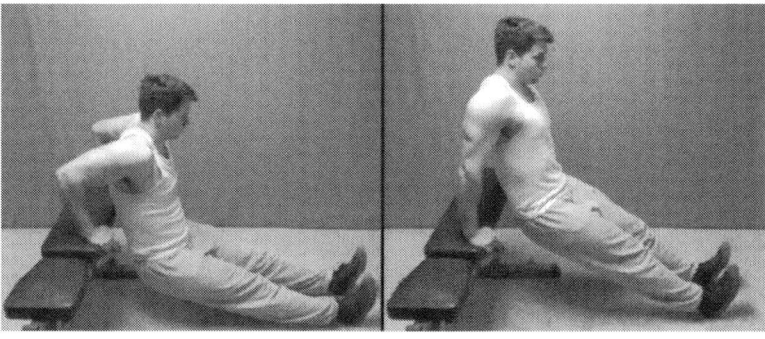

Variation: Feet up bench dip:

Make the bench dip tougher by raising your feet. This will also grant you a greater range of movement.

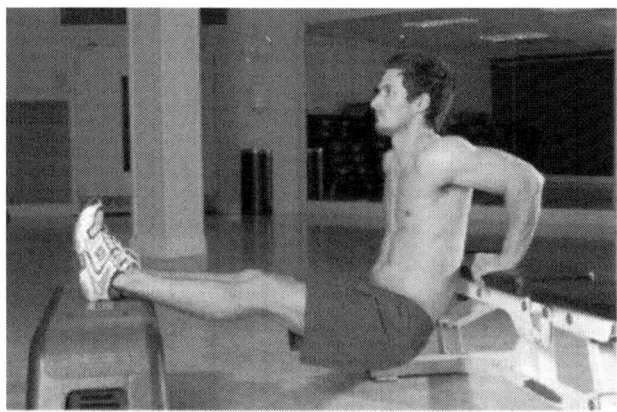

Step 1: Keep your feet at same altitude as your hips.

Step 2: Keep a firm grasp on the bench at all times or you could fall.

Variation: Weighted bench dip:

CALISTHENICS

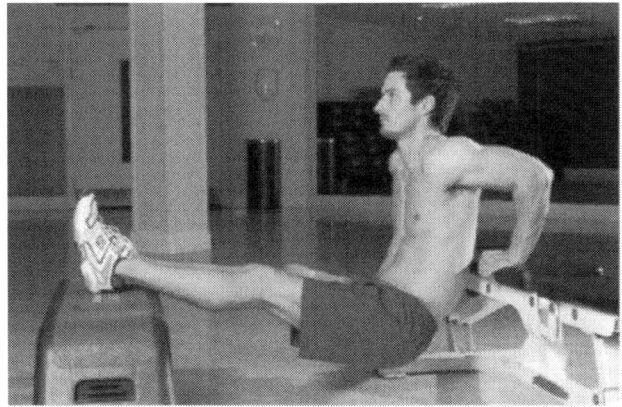

Lay a weight plate on your lap.

Variation: Bench dip with leg lift:

Step 1: As you lower, lift one leg off the floor.

Step 2: Alternate legs with each rep.

4. Toe Touch Sit Ups

This is a powerful exercise for your abs.

- Sit down and rock back pulling your legs in the air.
- Then, raise your arms wrinkling your elbows slightly.
- Lower and pull your legs in the air, letting your arms touch your toes as close as possible. If you can just touch the ankles that is fine. You can also lay your arms on the floor if raising them in the air is too much of a task for you. If you want, you can lay flat on the floor and elevate your arms to legs as you sit up.

Muscles Worked:

This crunch precisely aims at the middle and upper rectus abdominis, generally known as the "abs", the external oblique, the outer muscle of the abdomen and the internal oblique, the middle muscle of the abdomen. Rectus abdominis is a muscle that runs vertically along the anterior wall of the abdomen. Apart from aiming at these major abdominal muscles, this exercise also includes the hip flexors, a group of muscles that helps to pull the legs upward.

5. Planks

This is one of the main exercises for your abs. It is slightly easier than holding the body up with just the hands.

- Lay the forearms on the ground with elbows aligned below the shoulders and arms parallel to the body.
- Squeeze your gluteus.
- Keep your body in a straight line from the top of your head through your feet.
- Tighten your core.
- Tuck your chin.
- Try to hold this body position for as long as you can.

CALISTHENICS

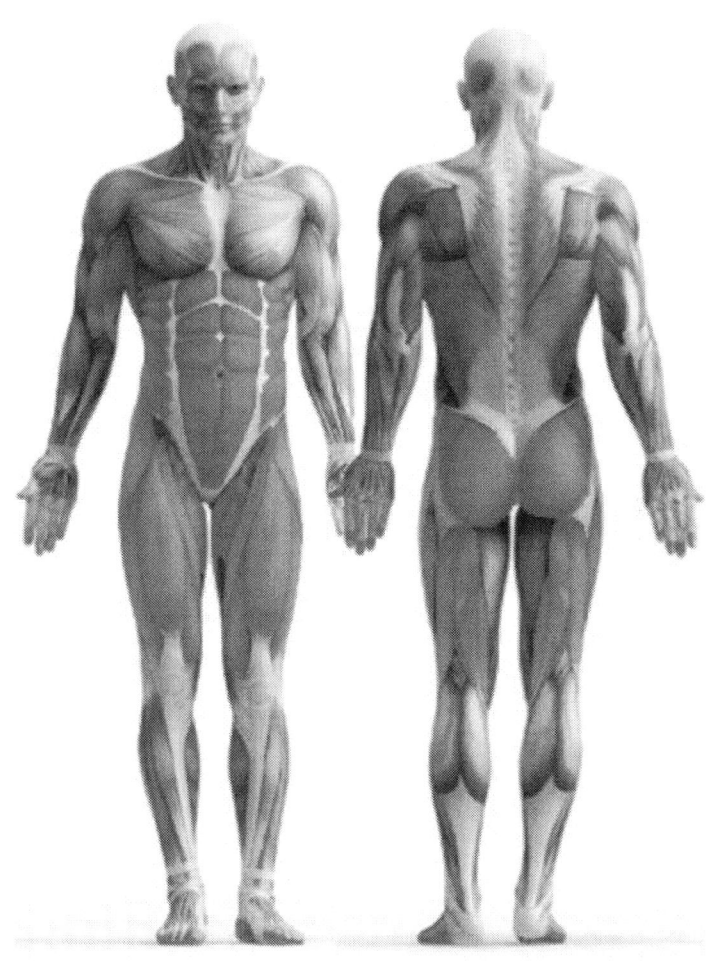

6. Supermans

- To start, lie straight and face down on the floor or workout mat. Your arms should be completely stretched in front of you. This is the starting position.

- At the same time elevate your arms, legs, and chest off of the floor and hold this contraction for 2 seconds.

Tip: Tighten your lower back to get optimum results from this workout. Remember to breathe out during this movement. Note: When holding the contracted position, you should look like superman when he is flying.

CALISTHENICS

- Gradually start lowering your arms, legs and chest back down to the starting position while breathing in.
- Repeat for the suggested number of repetitions prescribed in your program.

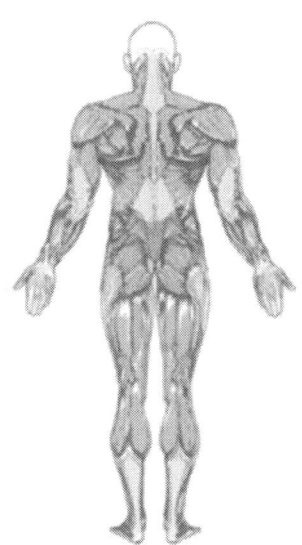

Variations: You can also do this exercise making use of one arm and leg at a time. Simply raise your left leg, arm and side of your chest and do the same with the right side.

7. Squats

The squat is one of the simplest bodyweight workouts you can do. They are easy to do, and thanks to the nature of the exercise, it can burn calories more rapidly than most other bodyweight exercises. This is because the squat works out your gluteus maximus, the quadriceps, the hamstrings, and finally, the erector spinae. Among these large muscle groups is the gluteus maximus, which is the largest muscle in your body, and by exercising them, you strain them against all of your upper body weight, repeatedly.

Let's progress to the form. As seen in the picture above, you begin by standing straight, with your feet spread about shoulder length apart. As you start bending your knees, visualize yourself sitting on a chair, once your femur (big thigh bone) is parallel to the ground, you should pause for one second, then slowly come back up. Keep in mind that, when performing bodyweight training, or calisthenics, you need to take your time. It may be challenging to get used to at first but once you are able to relax, and focused on the exercise, taking your time with each and every rep, you'll come to prefer it that way and you'll work the muscles a lot harder.

CALISTHENICS

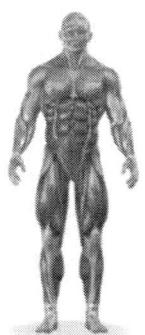 

Squat

Quadriceps
Gluteus Maximus
Adductor Magnus
Soleus
Hamstrings
Gastrocnemius
Erector Spinae
Rectus Abdominis
Obliques

8. Single Arm Plank

The one-arm improved plank is a calisthenics and pilates exercise that mostly targets the abs and to a lesser degree also targets the shoulders and hip flexors.

There are several different one-arm modified plank variations that you can try out that may need dissimilar types of one-arm modified plank equipment or may even require no equipment at all.

The one-arm modified plank is an exercise for those with a beginner level of physical fitness and exercise experience.

- ***Step 1:*** Get down on your hands and knees and make your body into a straight line.
- ***Step 2:*** Lift your feet up off the ground.
- ***Step 3:*** Take your right hand off the ground so that all the weight is on your left arm.
- ***Step 4:*** Hold this position for the desired amount of time and then switch hands.

CALISTHENICS

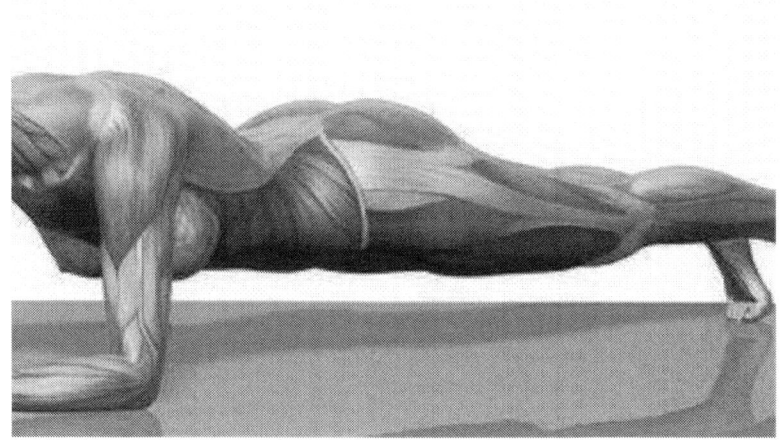

9. Bridge

When most people think of bridges, they think of a short bridge, which is the most common type of bridge and the one that you'll most probably see at any basic gym.

But even though this form of the bridge is great for those with a feeble or injured lower back, it's fairly non-taxing for anyone who has been working out extremely for a while, so they speedily skip over any other forms of the exercise, believing it's too easy for them.

But here's the thing: half bridges are by no means the most challenging form of the exercise. And if almost anyone, including those who regard themselves as pretty strong, did attempt the ultimate bridge - the stand to stand bridge - they'd almost be certain to fall due to lack of strength of flexibility.

Practicing bridges consistently will:
- Help dispose of back pain triggered by sitting hunched over all day long.
- Secure the spine in preparation for weighty or explosive movements.
- Strengthen your spinal muscles, which can stop slipped discs.

- Give the total front of your body an incredible stretch.
- Result in extra stamina in sports and life.
- Train every single muscle in your back - as well as nearly every other muscle in your body.

Begin wherever your current level is, then work up to the tougher variations as your strength and flexibility increases. Target training bridges 2-3 times a week - but even once a week will make you stronger and more flexible.

Short bridges

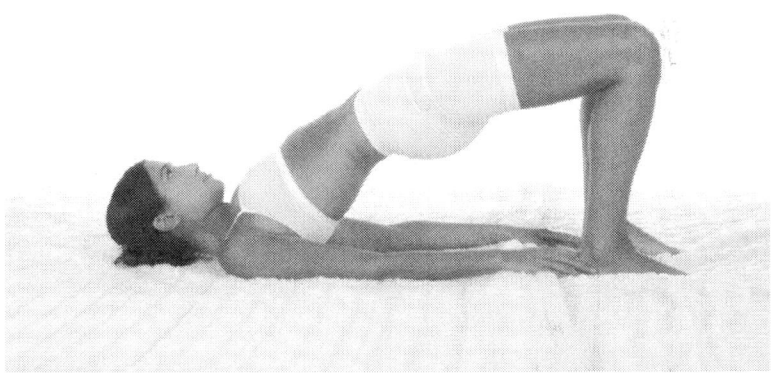

Short bridges are ideal for beginners or people with former back injuries. They gradually work your back, butt, and hamstring muscles and are an idyllic starting place.

How to do them: Lay on your back with your knees bent. Tighten your butt and abs and elevate your butt and hips as high as you can while still keeping your shoulders on the ground. Hold for one second, then lower down.

Do it: Two sets of 20-25 reps 2-3 times a week.

Straight bridges

Straight bridges are the following advancement in the bridge exercise, and will begin working your shoulders as well as your back, butt and leg muscles.

How to do them: Lay on your back with your legs straight. Put your hands on the floor on the outside of your hips, pointing your fingers toward your toes. Push yourself up onto your hands, raising the hips up and tightening your butt as you do so. Hold for a second, then lower back down.

Do it: Two sets of 20-25 reps.

Elevated bridges

Elevated bridges are the next step to aid you facilitate into doing complete bridges. These really start working your shoulders as well as your back, butt and leg muscles.

How to do them: Locate a bench or elevated surface that's about knee height or higher (make sure it's sturdy) and sit in front of it. Face away from the bench, then place your hands by your head with your fingers pointing toward your feet. Press through your hands and elevate your hips, arching your back and stretching your arms. Raise your hips as high as you can, then lower back down.

Do it: Two sets of 15 reps.

Full bridges

Full bridges work almost every muscle in your body, and will get you a crazy strong and flexible back. Plus, they're just fun.

How to do them: Lay on your back on the floor with your knees bent and your hands at the sides of your head, fingers pointing toward your toes. Push your hips up, rounding your back and tightening your butt, abs and leg muscles as you do this. Push through your shoulders so everything gets a good stretch, and deeply respire. Hold for one second, then lower back down.

Do it: Two sets of 15 reps.

Bridge walk downs

Bridge walk downs are the primary step in the development toward stand to stand bridges. They can be a little scary at first, but you'll soon learn to trust yourself adequately to know that you won't fall!

How to do them: Stand a few feet from a wall with your back facing the wall. Lean backward, rounding your back and tightening your butt until your hands hit the wall. Gradually walk your hands down the wall as far as you can. Your objective should be to reach the ground to get into a complete bridge. Once you reach the ground, simply sit down, stand back up and do it again.

Do it: Two sets of 10 reps.

Bridge walk ups

Bridge walk ups are considerably tougher than walk downs, so don't get too discouraged the first time of trial. Walk ups are an essential step in training for stand to stand bridges.

How to do them: Stand a few feet from a wall with your back facing toward the wall. Lean backward, rounding your back and squeezing your butt until your hands hit the wall. Slowly walk your hands down the wall until you're in a complete bridge. Make use of your hands to walk back up the wall, squeezing your butt and pushing your hips slightly forward to get you away from the wall and standing up again. That's one rep.

Do it: Two sets of 8 reps.

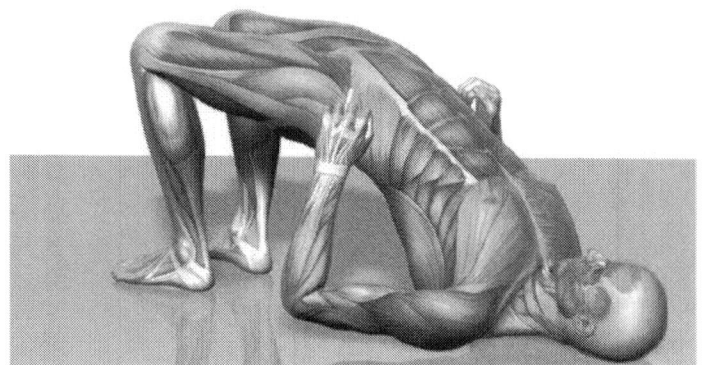

10. Leg Raise

Done properly, leg raises are the "go to" way to strengthen your core in calisthenics exercises. All of the following movements can also be performed while lying on the ground, but with decreased muscle use in the lower back and arms.

Knee Raises:

As a good progression exercise, the knee raise develops the core strength necessary in order to complete the standard leg raise. To perform this move, hold the bar in a standard pronated grip and tense your core while lifting your knees up to your chest. Focus on performing a slow and controlled movement. For added difficulty, try to perform a pelvic tilt at the end to elevate your hips slightly higher. Another modification could be to rotate the torso to one side to focus more on the oblique muscles.

Leg Raises:

For those that do not have the flexibility for the 180 degree leg raise, intermediate leg raises will help develop the core, back, and forearm strength required for the next progression. To do these, simply grip the bar like you would a standard pull up and bring your legs to a 90 degree angle while bending at the hip. It is important to keep your legs straight, as doing so will get the most out of those lower abs. Focus on performing a slow and controlled movement with no rocking back and forth. Also, resist arching your back, as it puts negative stress on the low back. To prevent this, contract the entire core throughout the exercise so that your hips remain in front of your body.

Muscles Groups Used: Abs, Lower Back, Hip Flexors

11. V Sits

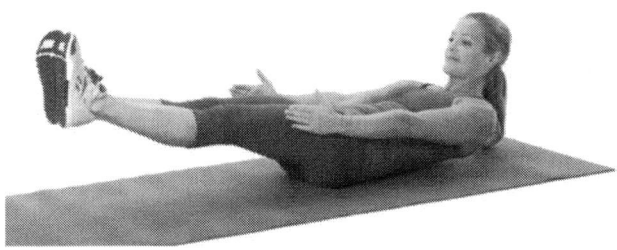

- Begin in a seated position with your knees bent and feet off the floor. Your chest should be open and lifted. This is comparable to a modified Boat pose in yoga.

- With your arms by your sides, gradually unfold from your seated v by lowering your torso and legs toward the floor at the same time. Halt when your legs are around a 45-degree angle, or when you feel your lower back arch away from the floor. Be certain to keep your head and shoulders off the floor and your lower back pressed into the mat.

- With your core tight and tucked, make use of your abs to return to the initial position.

- Repeat for one minute. Keep your abs engaged as you do this move, instead of depending on gravity; if it gets too difficult, then keep your knees bent as you lower down.

This is not a simple abdominal move, since it involves total body strength and control. This exercise should be done only after you have warmed up. The key is to evade pushing out your stomach by working your deep abs by pulling your navel to your spine. If you find your posture weakening, keep your knees bent.

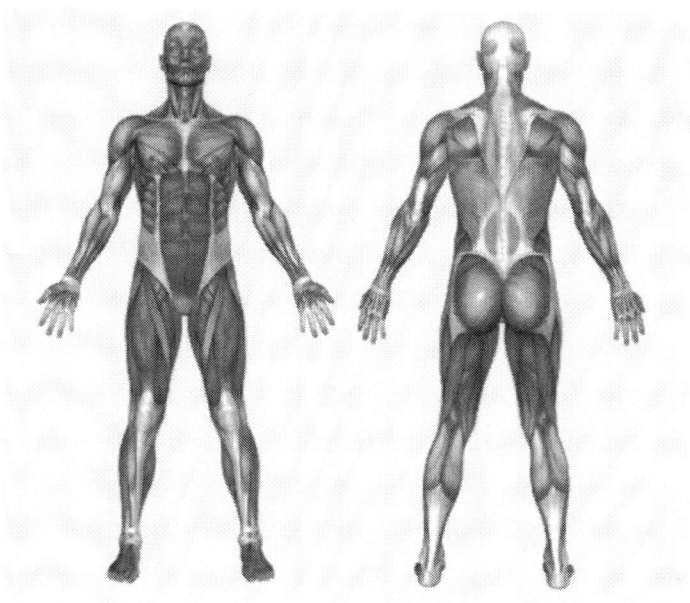

12. In And Out Squat Jumps

Squat jumps in and out increase lower body power and coordination. The movement targets the quads, hamstrings, glutes, and calves.

- Stand with your feet together, putting your hands in front of you on your thighs.
- Bend your legs, jump, and separate your feet in mid-air.
- Land with feet wider than shoulder-width apart, lowering into a squat. Jump out of the squat and land back in the initial position, bringing your feet together on landing.

Trainer's Tips:

- Make sure to jump as high as possible.
- Do not land with force. Use the balls of your feet to cushion the impact.
- Do not let your knees curve inward when jumping from the wider posture.

13. Mountain Climbers

If you are fresh to mountain climbers do the knee to chest motion slow and steady then build it up to a more rapid pace with practice. If you are more advanced try placing your hands on a raised platform such as a step as this will make the mountain climber more challenging.

- Adopt a press up position so your hands are directly under your chest at shoulder width apart with stretched arms.//
- Your body should form a straight line from your shoulders to your ankles.
- Raise your right foot off the floor and gradually elevate your knee as close to your chest as you can.
- Return to the initial position and repeat with your left leg.
- Continue switching for the desired number of reps or time.

14. Wide Grip Pull Ups

- Grip the pull-up bar with your palms facing forward making use of the wide grip. Your hands need to be spread out at a distance wider than your shoulder width.

- As you have both arms stretched in front of you holding the bar at the wide grip width, take your torso back around 30 degrees or so while forming a curvature on your lower back and sticking your chest out. This is your beginning position.

- Pull up your torso until the bar touches your upper chest by drawing the shoulders and the upper arms down and back. Breathe out as you perform this portion of the movement. *Tip*: Lay emphasis on squeezing the back muscles once you attain the full contracted position. The upper torso should remain motionless as it moves through space and only the arms should move. The forearms should do no work other than hold the bar.

- After a second on the contracted position, start breathing out and slowly lower your torso back to the starting position when your arms are completely extended and the lats are fully stretched.

Variations:
- If you are new to this exercise and do not have the ability to perform it, use a chin support machine if available. These machines use weight to aid you push your bodyweight.

- Or else, a spotter holding your legs can help.
- Alternatively, more improved lifters can add weight to the exercise by using a weight belt that allows the addition of weighted plates.
- The behind the neck variation is not advised as it can be hard on the rotator cuff as a result of the hyperextension formed by bringing the bar behind the neck.

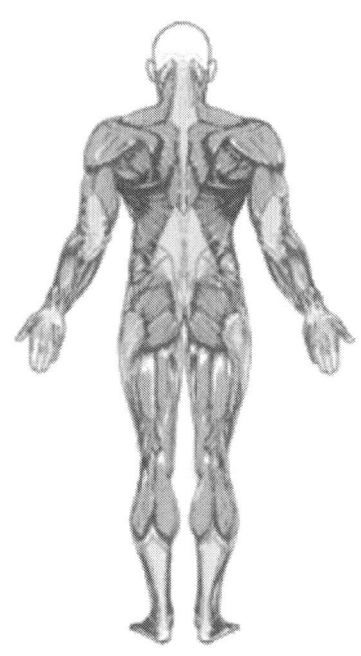

15. Crunches

The basic crunch is the perfect abdominal exercise in a strength-training program. Pay particular attention to your form when you do crunches, principally if you have lower-back or neck problems.

- Lay on your back with your knees bent and feet flat on the floor, hip-width apart.
- Place your hands at the back of your head so that your thumbs are behind your ears.
- Don't cord your fingers together.
- Hold your elbows out to the sides but rounded slightly in.
- Tilt your chin a little, allowing a few inches of space between your chin and your chest.
- Slightly pull your abdominals inward.
- Curl up and forward so that your head, neck, and shoulder blades are lifted off the floor.
- Hold for a moment at the top of the movement and then lower slowly back down.

Tips for doing crunches:

- Keep your abdominals pulled in so you feel more tautness in your abs and so you don't overarch your lower back.

- Don't pull on your neck with your hands or draw your elbows in.

- Do curl as well as lift. In other words, don't tug your head, neck, and shoulder blades off the floor: you also need to curl forward, as if you're doubling over. Think of carrying your ribs to your pelvis and breathe out as you crunch up; breathe in as you lower back down, keeping your navel drawn in.

- Do slow and controlled crunches, doing 12 reps.

16. Lunge

The lunge is a calisthenics exercise (done without weights) aiming at the gluts, quads, and hamstrings. Lunges will enhance definition to your legs when correctly done, but when you perform them wrongly they can injure your joints. Right form makes any calisthenics exercise efficient and sometimes challenging, but it should not cause any pain or needless stress on your joints.

How to Perform a Traditional Basic Full Lunge:

- Start by standing with feet shoulder-width apart and then step forward (on either leg).

- First step with your heel in order to support your body-weight. The foot should point forward.

- When the front foot reaches a desired distance in front of you, begin to "genuflect" the back knee.

- This prompts the front knee to bend and your back foot will be on its toes. Take it easy as you may need to stabilize yourself while going down.

- Continue "genuflecting" until the back knee is inches off the ground and the front knee is at 90 degrees and directly above the toes. Do not go any extra than 90 degrees for the front leg.

- Raise yourself back to the original position using both legs and repeat the exercise for the opposite leg.

Be mindful that your back and neck MUST remain straight and perpendicular to the ground throughout the whole exercise. The arms may be placed at the sides, or next to the head, or held straight out to the sides as an isometric exercise so long as it does not hinder any of the form above.

Various Forms of Lunges:

There are several forms lunges for both beginners and regular athletes. We will attempt to name the most popular and effective ones. Here are some starter lunges which are also relaxed on the knees:

- **Assisted Lunge** - With the use of a chair to help you perform a traditional full lunge. You can also use a wall or anything that will help you keep stable. Lay emphasis on your form and technique with this.
- **Half-Lunge** - Adopt the same form and technique as the traditional lunge but you do not go all the way down with your back knee. Go halfway! Like the aided lunge, use this to focus on proper lunge form.

Attempt all the lunges above to get comfortable with the motion, form, and technique of a lunge before executing a full lunge.

Various Full-Lunges:

- **Long Lunge** - Increase the space between your feet. This focuses on the gluts. However, remember to not go any extra than 90 degrees with that front leg! You may not notice you're front leg going beyond 90 degrees so don't forget!
- **Short Lunge** - Decrease space between your feet. This focuses on the quadriceps. With this exercise, you may have an inclination to bring the front knee too far over the front toes, but don't!
- **Reverse Lunge** - Same principles as traditional basic full lunge but you start the exercise by stepping backwards with a leg.
- **Walking Lunge** - Same principle as traditional basic lunge but you continue to step forward each time you bring the front foot forward.
- **Straight Leg Lunge** - This will seem conversant to those in Pila-

tes. Step forward with a foot without bending the front knee more than 90 degrees, your back leg will stay totally straight without bending the knee to the ground. Your back will be straightened with the back leg - implying you will be leaning forward. You can place your arms on the floor for stability as long as it does not disrupt the form.

- **Elevated Front Foot Lunge** - Same procedure and skill as traditional lunge but the front foot is placed on a raised surface. It may seem simpler than a normal lunge, but it is a bit more challenging. This is best performed on stairways or steps. It is sometimes referred as the Split-Squat Lunge. It is typically done without alternating the legs for a set of reps.
- **Elevated Back Foot Lunge** - Think the reverse of the elevated front foot lunge. Take note that with this exercise, since the back foot is raised, clearly, the back knee may not be capable of going all the way down to inches off the floor. Don't go too far down! Also, recall the front foot does not bend more than 90 degrees! Also known as a Reverse Split-Squat Lunge.
- **Sliding Lunge** - You will be "sliding" your foot to do a reverse lunge in place of taking a step back. Use a towel or piece of cardboard etc. to carry out this exercise.

There are several other types of lunges but these will certainly give you a good solid workout. Keep in mind that form and technique are crucial with this calisthenics exercise!

Common mistakes with Lunges:

- Twisting your front knee "more" than 90 degrees – Don't! Your knee should not be at any acute angle smaller than 90 degrees. This leads to a lot of stress on your knee joint. 90 degrees should be the maximum angle of your front leg.

- Front knee spreads over the toes of the same leg – This goes together with the above problem. Your front knee should only go directly over your toes at the bottom of the exercise.

- Back knee should not point anywhere except straight down. It may be tough to stabilize yourself, but this is very significant so you don't injure your knee. If you must, do assisted lunges to warm up or start out so you don't injure yourself.

- Leaning forward or bowing when stepping forward – You need to keep your back vertical to the ground for proper form throughout the exercise! (unless noted otherwise).

- Locking knees at the top of the exercise (start position) – they should be ever-so-slightly bent to keep the all the muscles in the workout involved throughout your set.

- Looking down – No! Look straight forward and keep your whole neck down to your thighs straight.

- Starting a lunge with your feet too close or too wide. Your perfect position would be about shoulder width apart.

- Back knee should be 1-2 inches off the ground when performing a correct full lunge (unless noted otherwise).

Don't be startled if you're gluts and quads are sore the next day! That's a good sign. You will frequently see more variations of lunges in Pilates or Yoga so be sure to do them correctly so you don't hurt yourself. Lunges are one of the best calisthenics exercises for your lower body so make sure you include them into your workout regime.

17. Calf Raises

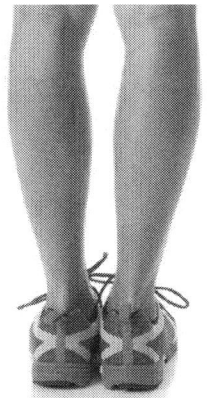 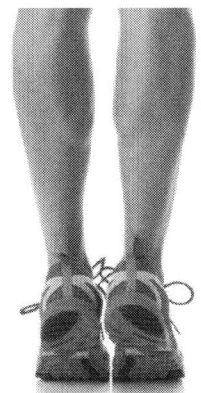

The calves are made up of many muscles, but the two main workhorses bodybuilders are concerned with are the gastrocnemius and the soleus. The gastrocnemius receives more stimulation with the knees spread out (standing calf raise) and the soleus with the knees bent (seated calf raise). That said, the soleus still receives some stimulation during a calf elevation even when the knees are extended.

The soleus has a better slow-twitch (ST) muscle fibre composition– up to 88%, one of the top ST compositions in the human body - and thus, more reps should be performed. Most traditional calf training routines, however, fail to generate adequate volume for this "endurance" muscle.

This is too bad, as a significant amount of volume at a decent force can result in hypertrophy. Lifting a substantial load, like your whole bodyweight, every day for a high number of reps will definitely put on muscle.

Since you're not making use of huge loads, this training can be accomplished every day, and it's the regularity that coaxes your body to adapt quickly. You'll be sore at first, but it won't be that bad.

Correct form is very important. Place your feet about shoulder-width apart and toes turned slightly out. Emphasize on raising the heels straight up as if they're puppet strings being pulled up by God himself.

Ensure that you contract hard at the top - visualize a double biceps pose, but for the fact that you're squeezing the hell out of your calves. Don't grasp on a wall or machine for support. The idea is not to unload in any manner, as we want those small stabilizers to grow as well. Just keep your arms at your sides or your hands on your hips.

You must be bare footed (no shoes). Make sure to elevate your heels as high as possible, and mete out your weight evenly over all your toes. Hold the top, contracted position for a full 2 seconds. It must be a certain stop at the top, and you must feel a peak contraction in the calves.

Following, control the lowering - don't just drop like a bomb! If you fail to do these two steps correctly, the rep is not significant. It's that easy. There must be quality repetitions to optimally profit from this type of training. The prime muscles will get hit, but so will all those little stabilizers, and in the long run, it will make a big change in the overall development of your calves.

18. Wall Sit

The wall sit is a calisthenics exercise that mainly targets the quads and to a lesser extent also targets the calves, gluteus, and hamstrings.

The only wall sit apparatus that you really need is the wall. However, there are many different wall sit variations that you can attempt that may require alternate types of wall sit equipment or may even require no equipment at all.

The wall sit is an exercise for those with an in-between level of physical fitness and exercise skill.

Step 1: Stand with your back flat against the wall and your feet about 1-2 feet away from the wall.

Step 2: Place your arms at your sides or across your chest.

Step 3: Bend at the knees and lower yourself until your thighs are parallel to the ground.

Step 4: Hold this position for the chosen time.

Tips:

- Your knees should produce a 90 degree angle between your upper and lower leg.
- Keep your hands at your side or across your chest. Do not place them on your knees.
- Keep your core and back tense throughout the movement.

Variations:

- Place your feet on a bosu ball and do the wall sit.
- Place the bosu ball between your back and the wall when doing the wall sit.
- Place a weight plate on your thighs to intensify the difficulty.

19. Jumping Jacks

This calisthenics exercise is to a certain extent plyometric in nature as it requires one to "jump," or hop slightly, to the side with your legs while raising the arms up.

- Start by standing with your feet close together, arms at your sides, and looking straight forward.

- Start by bending your knees a little and making use of the balls and toes of your feet, jump/hop outwards with your legs landing to the sides - right leg goes right, left leg goes left in a uniform motion. Go out as far as you are at ease with your legs, but usually the exercise is done with your legs going wider than shoulder width.

- With regard to your arms, as you begin jumping/hopping, raise your arms to the sides and proceed upwards to perform a full 180 degree motion. When your arms reach 180 degrees, your hands should clap at the top while your feet have just finished the jump/hop to the sides.

- Bend your knees and push off the balls and toes of your feet to jump/hop back to the original position.

- Your arms will return down to the side of your body as you get back to the original position.

- Rinse and repeat!

- That's it!

Various forms of the jumping jack:

- **Plank Jumping Jacks** – This is not done while standing but while adopting a push up position. Your shoulders should be over your wrists for good stability and balance for this exercise. Your feet start together and you jump/hop out to the sides with your legs further than shoulder width. Land on the balls and toes of your feet. Hop back to original position. Involve your abs for added effect! Do not lock your knees or elbows while performing this workout.

- **Power Jumping Jacks** – This is a more tense jumping jack that will entail much more athleticism. It is usually practiced for speed training and muscle strength. Adopting most of the steps of a traditional jumping jack, the exception is that it is done all in the air and you do not land on your feet once you jump/hop out to the sides. You may bend your knees a little further with the power jumping jack than the traditional jumping jack so that once you are airborne, you spread your legs to the side and bring them back to the original position very rapidly – all in the air. You extend your back and spine simultaneously as you lift yourself into the air – also clapping your hands at the end 180 degree motion of your arms. Land on the ball and toes of your feet together and arms to the side.

Common mistakes with jumping jacks:

- Locking the knees - Don't! Knees should be bent just a little while performing the exercise in its entirety.
- Avoid rounding the back and popping the knees out.
- Breathing - while jumping up exhale, while coming back to original position inhale.
- Look forward!
- You can go as fast as you want! Just recall form!

Jumping jacks have always been an effective calisthenics exercise reason why it is also still used in the military!

20. Jack Knife

- Lay flat on the floor (or workout mat) on your back with your arms stretched straight back behind your head and your legs extended as well. This will be your starting position.

- As you breathe out, bend at the waist while raising your legs and arms at the same time to meet in a jack-knife position. *Tip*: The legs should be extended and raised at approximately a 35-45 degree angle from the floor and the arms should be extended and parallel to your legs. The upper torso should be off the floor.

- While breathing in, lower your arms and legs back to the starting position.
- Repeat for the suggested number of repetitions.

Variation: If you are really advanced you could make use of a medicine ball for additional resistance.

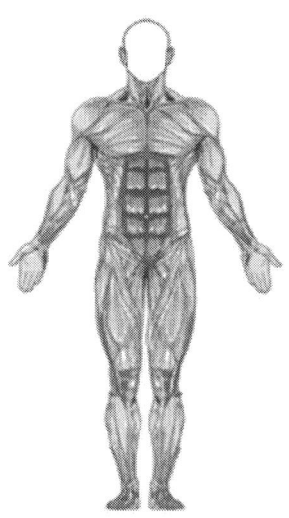

21. Curls

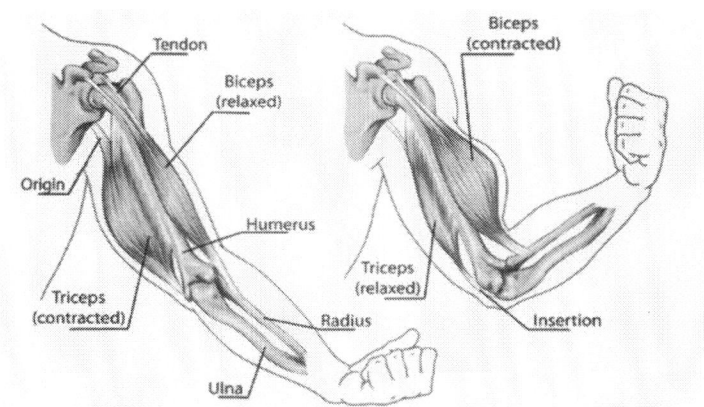

Bicep curls can be done with or without weights based on your choice. Any heavy object that aids in providing resistance can be used as a weight for this purpose. Resistance bands can also offer the necessary tension to increase the toughness of this exercise.

- Place your arms down at your sides, then curl them up toward you, bending your arm at the elbows.

- Lower the arm back to the starting position and repeat as required.

- Time your breathing, breathing in when you lift and breathing out as you lower your arm for better results.

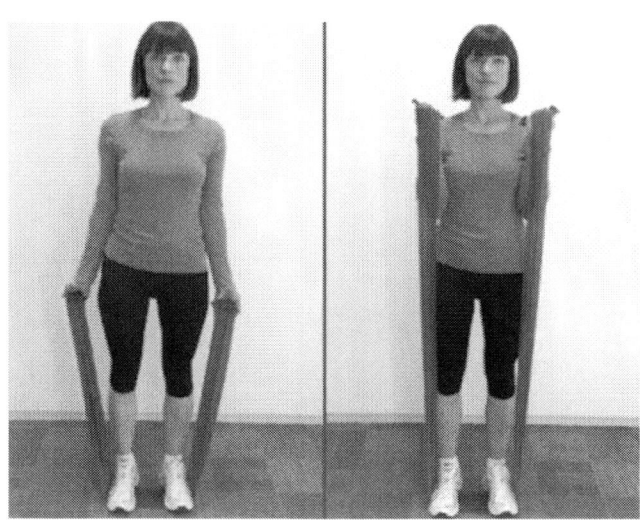

22. Tuck Jump

The tuck jump is a plyometrics and calisthenics workout that primarily aims at the quads and to a lesser extent also targets the calves, gluteus, and hamstrings.

- **Step 1:** Stand on flat surface that is softened (to lessen the wear on your legs and knees). Feet about hip-width apart.
- **Step 2:** Start the exercise by getting down into a half squat position and exploding off the ground while bringing your knees as close to your chest as possible. Swing arms upward as you blast off the ground.
- **Step 3:** Attempt landing softly on the balls of your feet with a bend in your knees and then explode back up straight away. Repeat this as many times as prescribed.

Tips:

Be sure to exhale as you explode off the ground and inhale on the way down. It is imperative that your take quick deep breaths during this exercise.

Try to land on the balls of your feet and as softly as possible.

Swing arms up as you jump to give yourself momentum.

Variations:

- Perform box jumps. Set a box about 6-inches in front of you and jump up on the box, landing on both feet.
- Perform with one leg. However, land with both feet on the ground, not one.
- Wear a weighted vest.

23. Bear Crawl

Stance: Hands and toes should touch the ground, and hips in the air.

- Move one leg and the opposite arm forward.
- Alternate by moving your other leg and opposite arm forward.
- Keep your hips high and back flat.

Variation: Practice by just taking a step or two at a time, slowly adding an additional step as the movement becomes easier.

CALISTHENICS

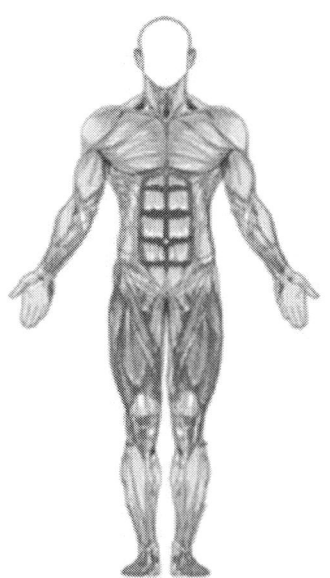

24. Step Up

This simple, but very effective exercise is best when done correctly.

The Step-Up for the legs is a great workout for leg development, single leg training, improving proprioception, and enhancing first step acceleration for athletes. Essentially, it is repeating the up phase of a squat or dead lift but on just one leg. Single leg training can be very advantageous for the prevention of injuries and asymmetry between the two legs. For numerous individuals this can be listed as a basic workout for them. Unfortunately, it is done wrong many times or with too heavy of weight and lack of emphasis.

Step-Up Tips:

- Find a plyo box or steady surface that you can stand safely on and when you have one foot on it, the height makes a 90 degree angle in the knee.
- You will stand in an erect postured position with the mid-section contracted for good balance.

- If you are holding weights in your hands (such as dumbbells or kettle bells) slightly pull back your shoulders (scapular retraction-pull the shoulder blades together in the upper back).

- When holding weight in your hands, squeeze hard your grasp as this will help retain good posture and limit any potential for momentum.

- With one foot placed totally on the box, press all your weight into the heel of that foot.

- As you come up be certain to maintain an upright posture and keep your knee back behind your toes all through the movement.

- Stand up on that foot until the leg is straight. Simultaneously, drive the other knee up in a high knee position so that the knee is above the hip.

- Maintain control and stability and either bring your leg down to the box or bring back the non-weight bearing foot back down to the ground.

- You can repeat on the same leg for the recommended reps or until form breaks down. You could also go into switching reps by bringing the weight bearing leg down and then step-up with the other leg.

This is great for several people as a standalone body weight workout before any additional weight. A weighted vest also works great. For more variation and difficulty use a barbell across the upper back in a back squat position. This is advanced and should only be done when you have mastered the step-up with dumbbells.

25. Donkey Kick

The donkey kick trains your lower back, core, legs and bottom. With each lift you are toning all 3 bottom muscles which makes this exercise a great substitute to the squat.

No equipment required for the donkey kick just some floor space and maybe a mat for your knees. It works your gluteus maximus, rectus abdominis, latissimus dorsi.

Variations:

- If you are not at ease with being on all fours then you can do this standing.
- Place both hands on the wall in front of you and one leg back and up as before, keeping the knee bent, lower and repeat on the opposite side.

Doing the Donkey Kick:

- Position on all fours so that your hands are shoulder width apart and your knees are straight below your hips.

- Bracing your abdominals and keeping your knee bent raise one leg up behind you until it is in line with your body and your foot is parallel to the ceiling.

- Lower back down to the initial position and replicate with the other leg.

26. Australian Chin Ups

This variation on the chin up comprises hanging below a bar that is set just above waist height while your heels touch the ground. You'll wind up at an angle that's closer to horizontal than vertical.

It puts slightly more focus on the rear delts and the muscles of your middle-back; muscles that may not be getting totally and thoroughly worked with regular pull-ups only. For those who are more advanced, try performing them as a superset right after a set of regular pull-ups. This is a great way to work towards increasing more reps to your pull-up total!

The Australian pull-up can be performed on any bar that is about waist height as long as it is firmly in place. The Smith machine is great for this exercise since it is able to be regulated (the higher the bar the simpler it will be - so start high if you're first learning) and safe. You can get imaginative with finding cool places to practice these and all types of pull-ups, just stay aware of your safety.

Trainer Tip:

The higher up the bar, the better the leverage. Definitely, this is only true up until a certain point-once the bar is too high, then you're just doing an ordinary pull-up!

Using the Australian in a Superset:

The Australian pull-up is a great workout to use as a superset with push-ups, as they train opposite muscle groups. You will get a great drive from doing this and it also allows you to keep your heart rate up. Due to the fact that you're letting certain muscles to rest while you are using others, you can maintain that increased heart rate without burning out your muscles too rapidly.

The Australian pull-up can also be used as a superset after the normal kind if you are trying to add your reps on pull-ups.

Plyometric Australian Pull-up:

You can transform the Australian pull-up into a plyometric exercise by alternating between overhand and underhand grips on alternating reps. You can also change back and forth from a wide grip to a narrow grip in an explosive fashion to mix up this workout with a plyometric spin.

The One Arm Australian Pull-up:

An Australian can definitely be done with just one arm. This is another technique to practice while building towards one arm pull-ups. The one arm Australian pull-up requires a ton of core strength and stability like any single limb movement. You can add an extra challenge by trying it on one leg also!

27. L-Sit

The L-sit is a classic isometric workout that works your whole body, focusing on the abdominal muscles. To be able to perform an L-sit, you'll need a strong core, strong arms and better than average flexibility in your hamstrings.

It's advised to learn the L-sit by practicing on parallel bars or push-up bars (even though you can practice this move with no equipment).

If you have bars, start by holding yourself upright, like you would at the top of a parallel bar dip. Then start raising your legs straight out in front of you until they are parallel to the ground. Your body will wind up looking like the letter "L" (hence "L-sit"). If you can't get to this position immediately, practice with your knees bent to work your way up to the full position.

Workouts such as planks and side planks are also a great way to help develop core strength. We recommend practicing them alongside or as a precursor to the L-sit. If your abs are strong and you're still having difficulties doing an L-sit, tight hamstrings might be what is stopping you. A regular stretching regimen can progressively loosen your hamstrings, but it will entail patience and diligence.

If you don't have bars or handles, you can attempt working your L-sit on the ground. Keep in mind that this is more difficult due to the fact that you have less freedom to lift into the hold.

Start with your palms flat or try bracing yourself up on your fingertips. Once you can hold a full L-sit for 30 seconds, you are prepared to advance to tougher core exercises like front levers, back levers and the infamous human flag.

Muscles Used: The L-sit is an isometric exercise, which implies it strengthens your body even though you're not moving. The L-sit works a variety of muscles throughout your body but targets your abs, arms – particularly your triceps – and hip flexors.

28. Russian Twist

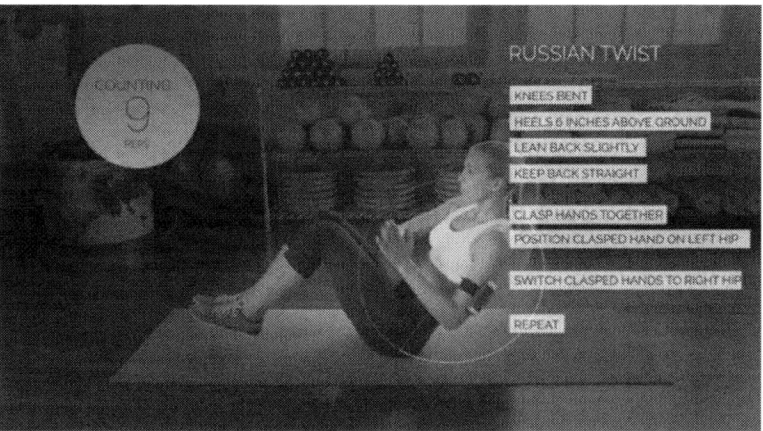

This exercise trains your oblique while most core exercises just work your midsection (abdominals) it also strengthens your back which in turn helps with keeping good posture. No equipment is needed for the Russian twist unless you want to add a weight so they can be done cheaply and anywhere there is a bit of space.

- Lay down on the floor putting your feet either under something that will not move or by having someone hold them. Your legs should be bent at the knees.

- Raise your upper body so that it produces an imaginary V-shape with your thighs. Your arms should be completely extended in front of you perpendicular to your torso and with the hands clasped. This is the starting position.

- Curl your torso to the right side until your arms are parallel with the floor while exhaling.

- Hold the tightening for a second and move back to the starting position while exhaling. Now move to the opposite side doing the same techniques you used to the right side.

- Replicate for the recommended number of repetitions.

CALISTHENICS

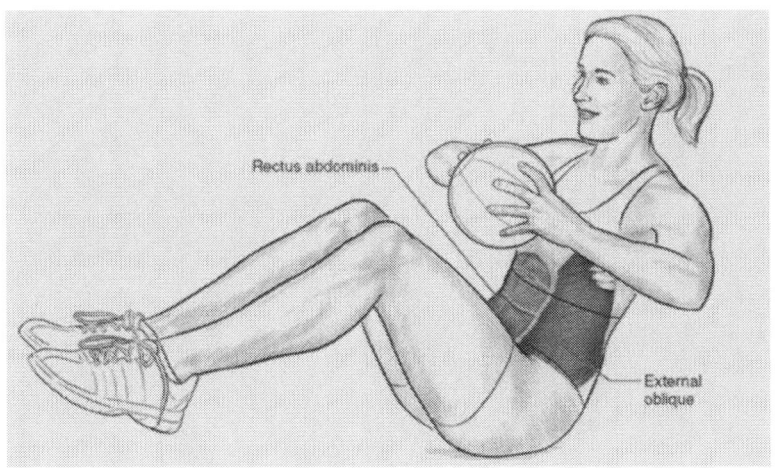

29. Bicycle

You can do normal crunches all day long, but that gets really boring for you and your abs. A great way to target the rectus abdominis and the oblique in one easy exercise is through bicycle crunches. Six-pack, here you come!

- Lay flat on the floor with your lower back pressed to the ground (pull your belly button in to target your deep abs as well).

- Put your hands at the back your head, then bring your knees in towards your chest and raise your shoulder blades off the ground, but be sure not to pull on your neck.

- Stretch out your right leg to about a 45-degree angle to the ground while turning your upper body to the left, bringing your right elbow towards the left knee. Make sure your rib cage is in motion and not just your elbows.

- Now swap sides and do the same motion on the other side to complete one rep.

CALISTHENICS

Speed is not the name of the game here: go gently to emphasize on your form and your respiration. It is unnecessary letting your elbows touch your knees as this could cause strain in your neck.

30. Reverse Crunch

The reverse crunch is a simple core strengthening exercise that also increases stability throughout the lower back, hips and spine. By starting the movement in your lower body and bringing your knees to your chest, you protect your back and create a greater range of motion, which can help put more tension on your abdominal muscles.

- Lay down on the floor with your legs fully extended and arms to the side of your torso with the palms on the floor. Your arms should be motionless for the entire exercise.
- Move your legs up so that your thighs are perpendicular to the floor and feet are together and parallel to the floor. This is the starting position.
- While breathing in, move your legs towards the torso as you roll your pelvis backwards and you elevate your hips off the floor. Your knees will be touching your chest at the end of this movement.

- Hold the contraction for a second and move your legs back to the starting position while breathing out.
- Repeat for the recommended number of repetitions.

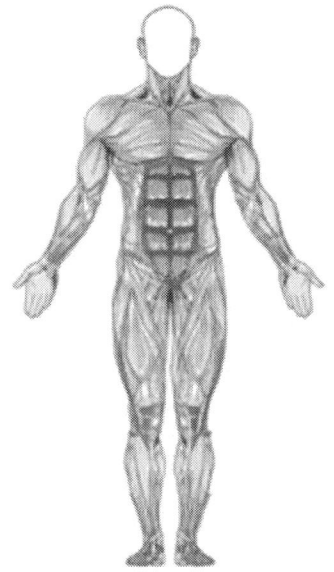

Now you have seen – and hopefully practiced – a set of the beginner exercises used in calisthenics workouts, it's time to look at the more complex moves for intermediate and expert moves.

There are a few online resources that can also help you with getting started that you might wish to check out at this stage: *Fit Body Buzz*, *Baristi Workout* and *Calisthenics Daily* to name just a few.

CHOOSING THE BEST EXERCISE PLAN FOR YOU

So how do go about picking the right exercises to produce the best results? This is of course very personalized to you and your goals. What works for some, won't suit another. Also, if you wish to lose weight, you aren't going to be working out the same as someone who wants to gain muscle. Workouts incorporating these exercises are looked at later in this book.

That being said, Bodybuilding.com has run a campaign, to get its readers to vote on their all-time favorite calisthenics exercises - the ones that *they* felt produce the best results, and here is what they discovered people preferred:

- Push ups
- Dips
- Chin ups
- Squats
- Lunges
- Crunches
- Calf Raises

Quality Vs Quantity

There is often a debate about exercise - whether quality or quantity is better. As you have probably guessed by now, calisthenics definitely works on the *quality* side of things and there has been a whole lot of scientific research to support this, as shown by **Fitness By Dr. Mercola** at fitness.mercola.com:

Endorsed exercise rules typically base their recommendations on the number of minutes or hours you should workout. But the latest research suggests this is an archaic approach.

The efficiency of your fitness program isn't measured by how long you exercise. It's measured by **the quality of your exercise**. In accordance to an out-of-date fitness doctrine, a person who jogs for 60 minutes would by theory be getting a "better" workout than someone who does a 20-minute workout… but this is a wrong over-generalization.

Research now demonstrates that some of the best workouts last only 20 minutes (or less), and that by including multi-dimensional movement, high-intensity exercise, recovery, and more into your routine, you can get a superior workout in a fraction of the time.

In fact, you can see by his research, calisthenics (or functional exercise) is actually the best way to work out. He has conducted numerous studies on the subject, including one with divided overweight or obese individuals into three groups. These groups then went on to consume 60 grams of protein powder a day. One group remained sedentary; one took part on intense resistance training and the other mixed cardio with strength training.

The final group, which used the most diverse range of exercises, showed the most improvement to their weight. They lost the most weight (2.6 percent) and fat mass (6.6 percent) while gaining the leanest body mass (two percent). The other groups did see a difference but nowhere near as significant.

The conclusion that Dr. Mercola drew from this is that functional exercises, which help the body perform real life activities, were the ones that had the most impact. A very important lesson that calisthenics athletes take on board.

Dr. Mercola's studies also go on to make the following, very important, points:

- *Exercising for too long can actually backfire* – Long periods of high endurance exercise can put unnecessary stress on your body and your heart.

- *Increasing intensity saves time* – It is also much more effective, as the longer recovery time allows for growth.

- *Proper recovery is crucial* – You stress your body out with exercise, so it has to be reiterated just how vital recovery and rest time is. Your body will give you clues into how it's feeling, and when it's telling you to rest – listen to it.

4 Little Known Exercise Techniques

There are a few techniques that you'll want to apply to your calisthenics exercises to ensure that you're getting the best quality out of them. These include:

Breathing

Getting your breath right whilst performing these exercises is very important.

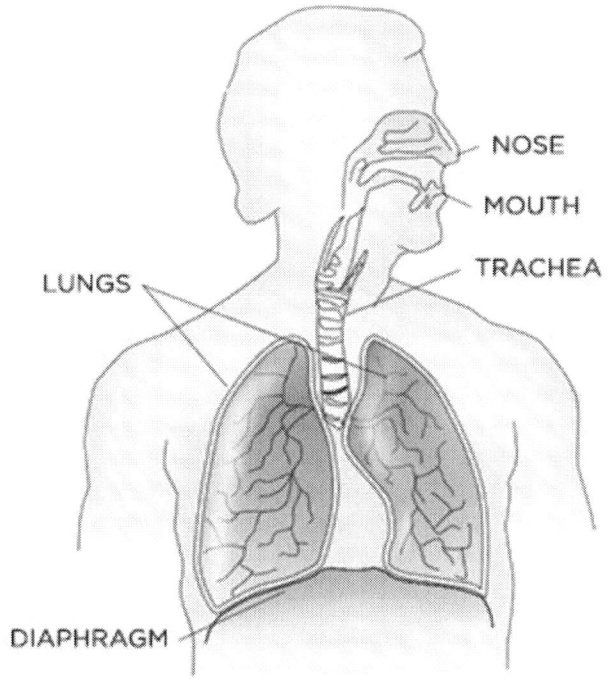

When performing any exercise, there will be muscles that do the bulk of the work, and ones that support this movement. No matter what it is that you're doing, your breath is *always* important, so it's absolutely essential that you get it right.

The following bullet points give you examples of how you can improve the way you breathe, also improving the way you exercise:

- ***Belly Breathing*** – Your diaphragm is the powerful muscle inside your body that controls your breath. Proper activation of your diaphragm draws the breath deep from within your stomach, not your chest. To practice belly breathing, stand upright and place a hand on your stomach. As you take a deep breath, expand your abdomen so that you can feel it. With enough practice, you'll be able to take a deep breath without your shoulders moving.
- ***Static Electricity*** – Once you have mastered belly breathing, you'll want to train yourself to exhale while deeply contracting your core from the inside. This is all to do with your throat. There is an opening in there, called the glottis. This prevents air from exiting your lungs, and can be used to seep air out as necessary. Do this, whilst tightening your abdomen. In fact, the best way to practice this is whilst performing static exercises.
- ***Waiting to Exhale*** – The *valsalva manoeuvre* is often used to help with bodyweight exercises, and consists of using your diaphragm to create a bubble of air in your belly, which stabilizes the trunk during heavy lifting. Just be careful, as waiting to exhale can cause fainting if not done correctly.

Trying out all of these techniques can help you build up your body's strength.

Speed

The speed you perform your exercises will increase as you develop. You need to be sure that you are pushing yourself to the absolute maximum in the 20 minutes exercise time (or whatever time *you* have personally set) so the you need to set the right speed for you, whilst allowing yourself to perform the exercise *fully* to get the most out of it.

As calisthenics is a high intensity exercise, you may wish to examine **speed reps**.

Speed training is comparable to plyometric training in that the movements are done fast and explosively. However, unlike plyometric, you do not get airborne when you do speed reps. In fact, when performing speed reps on workouts like pull-ups and dips that involve gripping a bar, it is recommended holding on tightly!

In addition, it can help to think about doing the negative portion of the rep as fast as possible, which will involve the antagonist muscles. This implies if I am doing speed pull-ups, I will think about pushing myself down away from the bar at the top of each rep.

Before trying speed reps of any exercise, be sure that you can first perform the exercise at a normal tempo with proper form. It's also a good idea to warm up thoroughly before this type of training.

The main point to take from this is that getting the movement right, before working on the speed that you perform them, is utterly essential.

Movements

Getting the right movements is very important to calisthenics. The Exercises guide in this book has given you step-by-step instructions on some of the most common exercises you will partake in.

Calisthenics Movement also has a lot of great advice for you, whatever level of expertise you are!

Focus

Focus can be considered to be the most essential principle for skill accomplishment. Focus can also be one of the trickiest to implement. For simpler implementation, focus could be categorized into 3 distinct categories:

1. **Short Term Focus** - Remain 100% focused on the movements as you perform them. Don't let your mind wander off somewhere else. This also counts for in between workout, as you'll want to be mentally prepared at all times.
2. **Midterm Focus** - Keep working towards a single plan for about 3 months. That way it'll be very difficult for your focus to trail off somewhere else. It's long enough to be a goal, but short enough not to give you time to get disheartened.
3. **Long Term Focus** - Your end goal needs to be in your mind all the time. If it isn't always there, bugging you, you'll never achieve what it is that you want.

Getting rid of distractions is a great way to keep you focused. There will always be things popping up, and getting in the way. It might be advisable to create a 'What Not To Do' list, to ensure that you know exactly what might crop up.

Maintaining Your Physique

Once you have developed the physique you want via calisthenics, you will want to maintain it. There is no point in working so hard to get what you desire, just to lose it and have to begin all over again!

There have been some studies which suggest that keeping up some level of exercise - even one day a week - can help you keep up your fitness levels and maintain your physique. As long as you are performing quality exercises correctly during that time, you will be fine. So it may be worth considering calisthenics as a lifestyle change, rather than simply another exercise plan!

Eating a balanced diet will also contribute to this, which is why this book has an entire guide for your eating in a later chapter.

Moving Up A Level

Once you've mastered the beginner calisthenics moves, there will come a time that you want to push yourself and try harder things. This isn't something to take lightly; there are a lot of factors to consider.

Principles of Progression

There are three main principles of progression that you need to understand to move forward. These are *Deconstruction*, *Progressive Resistance* and *Consistency*. We will look at these in more detail.

Deconstruction:

Deconstruction is one of the most important principles of progression. It focuses on exploring the calisthenics move, that you've performed, from start to finish, and seeing what you can learn from that.

An easy way to do this is to get someone to take a photograph of you performing a move, and critically examining it. Be as attentive as possible. Even the smallest detail can make a big difference. Note what you have gotten exactly right and what you need to work on. Perfection is the end aim.

A great example of this, can be seen with this image of a planche. To deconstruct it, go from the toe to the head and make notes:

1. His feet are pointing away with toes.
2. His body is in a perfectly straight line, which is vital for this move.
3. His shoulders are pushed all the way to the front.

4. His arms are straight, with his elbows locked. This is the best way to perform this move.
5. His fingers are pointed forward, which means that he is standing more on his fingers rather than on the full palm. They are also placed right under his centre of gravity.
6. He looks forward as he performs the planche.

These are the kind of notes that you need to be making for your deconstruction.

Progressive Resistance:

Progressive resistance is breaking down the difficult task ahead (for example, improving a move, or moving up a level) into severable manageable tasks. Sequence these in an order that makes sense to you - maybe easiest to hardest.

After you have deconstructed your photograph, and worked out what you need to do next, the parts that you need to work on, and figure out *exactly* how you're going to do that. You will also want to set a timeline of *when* you want to achieve this. Of course, as you're trying to improve, you will get into a cycle of deconstruction and progressive resistance, until you get it right.

Consistency:

You will need to work at calisthenics moves consistently to get them right. Without the right amount of dedication, you're setting yourself up for failure. Patience will work alongside this consistency as not everything will be easy, all of the time.

Methods of Progressing in Bodyweight Exercises

Here are some other very useful tips in progression with calisthenics:

- **Increase range of motion** - When a move starts to become easy for you, change the way that you do it, to make it difficult for you - when something doesn't challenge you anymore, chances are it isn't doing a lot for you.
- **Add weight** - If you struggle to add time to a move, add weight to make it more taxing.
- **Change body position** – If you can perform a move easily on the floor, try including obstacles. Do it off the couch or the wall, or find something that works for you.
- **Combining difficult and easier exercises** – If you're struggling to get to where you want to be, right away, try mixing the hard with the easy. You'll progress without getting frustrated or causing yourself any damage.

10 INTERMEDIATE EXERCISES

Here is a selection of intermediate level exercises for you to try (when the time is right for you).

1. Diamond Push Ups

The diamond push up is an advanced progression of the standard push-up which increases the demands on the triceps and shoulders.

- Assume the standard push up position with your hands together directly beneath your chest so that index fingers and thumbs touch to form a triangle or "diamond" shape.

- Slowly lower your body to the ground keeping your core tight. Be sure to keep your elbows tucked in close by your sides in order that they make a 45-degree angle with your torso. Without changing your hand placement, halt and push yourself back to the starting position.

Tips:

- Do not place your hands very far in front of you. Your chest should touch the triangle at the bottom of the push up.

- Avoid moving hips out of position. Instead, keep your core tight and back flat throughout the movement.

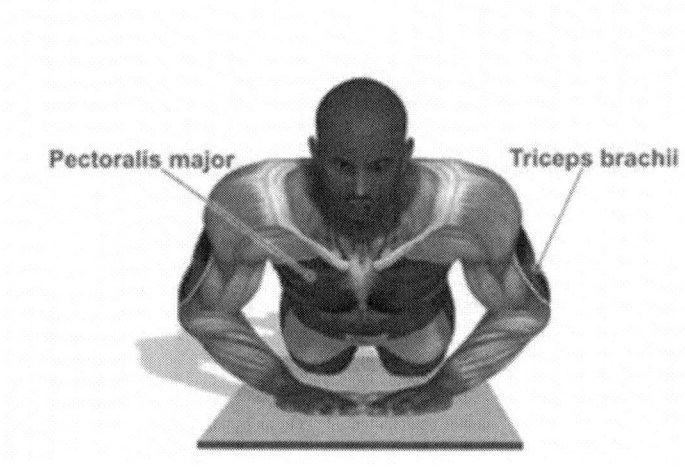

2. Superman Push Up

The push up is part of the most versatile strength exercises because you can tweak your hand and feet placement to intensify difficulty and focus on specific muscles. The Superman push up is an extremely difficult exercise that requires a high level of core and upper body strength. The traditional push up works the chest, shoulders and triceps, but due to the different hand placement, the Superman push up works different muscles.

Getting Prepared:

The traditional push up involves placing your hands on the floor so that they're positioned just outside your torso and level with your chest. The Superman push up, however, entails you to lie on your stomach and stretch your arms out in front of you so that your hands are placed beyond your head and at shoulder-width apart. With your legs and arms fully extended, set your toes and palms against the floor to prepare for the exercise.

Exercise Execution:

Lift your torso and thighs off the floor by pushing your palms and toes into the floor. Your body will rise up no more than 12 inches off the floor. Control your body back to the floor and then go into the next repetition. Your torso and thighs should stay straight and your legs and arms should remain fully extended throughout the entire exercise.

Muscles Worked:

The Superman push up doesn't primarily work your chest, shoulders and triceps like the traditional push up. Instead, it challenges your latissimus dorsi, which is the broadest muscle in your back. Your latissimus dorsi is responsible for extending your arms behind you. As you push your hands into the floor, your lats are attempting to drive your arms back. The pectoralis major in your chest does contribute to shoulder extension. In addition, your abdominals, obliques and hip flexors isometrically work to keep your torso in a straight line and prevent it from collapsing it to the floor as you lift and lower your body.

3. Pull Up Progression

There are a lot of advanced moves in the pull up progression.

Overview: Pull ups train the muscles in your upper back (the latissimus dorsi, and the trapezius), in your shoulders (the anterior deltoids), and in your arms (the biceps and brachialis). The closer together the hands are placed, the more focus is on the biceps. The further they are, the more emphasis on the lats. Definitely, pull ups will also examine your grip strength.

Form: Pull ups are typically done with your hands facing away from you, while chin ups are carried out with your hands facing towards you (and chin ups also focus on the biceps more). Between the two, chin ups are generally regarded to be the slightly easier version. See chin ups illustration below.

About the progression: Changes between the first few variations are difficult in this progression. However, the horizontal pulls progression works like muscles to pull ups, and it has a much gentler gradient. The two greatly benefit from each other.

Select one of the following variations as a start point and do 3 sets of between 4 and 8 repetitions with periods of between 1 and 2 mins of rest between each set. When you can perform 3 sets of 8, proceed to the next exercise in the progression.

1. Leg assisted pull ups

Position a chair under your pull up bar, and support yourself with one leg as you pull your body up. What is of importance here is that you control how much help you get from your support leg. Try reducing this support with time. This can be done by putting just the tip of your toes on the chair under you.

2. Jackknife pull ups

Place a high object in front and under your pull up bar (a strong chair or better yet a table). Placement is vital for jackknife pull ups to be effective: ideally, the table or chair should be sufficiently high for your legs to rest on it at 90 degrees or less to your torso, with your waist bent. Push with your heels into the chair or table and straighten your waist while taking your chin to the bar.

3. Eccentric pull ups

Jump up in the pull up position with your chin above the bar, then gradually lower yourself down to the count of 5 seconds.

4. Half pull ups (top half)

Begin in mid-range, and pull up yourself through half the range of movement, until your chin clears the bar. At that point, lower yourself back to mid-range (elbows bent at 90 degrees).

5. Pull ups

From a dead hang, pull up yourself until your chin clears the bar.

6. Close grip pull ups

Similar to pull up, but with your hands close together. This disparity lays added emphasis on your biceps.

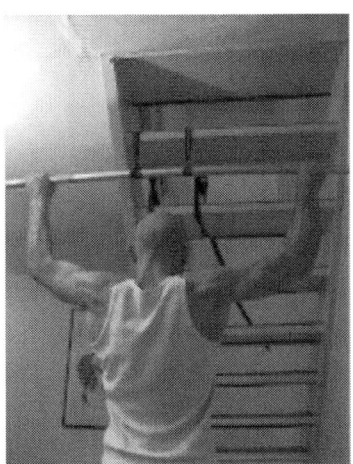

7. Wide grip pull ups

Similar to pull up, but with your hands wider than shoulder width apart. This variation lays additional emphasis on your latissimus dorsi.

8. Archer pull ups

Emphasize on pulling with one arm, with negligible support from the other. The other arm should gently straighten over the bar in the course of the pulling motion. Only go up to 6 on each arm, interchanging each arm, rather than the 8 reps the basic routine calls for. This discrepancy of pull ups is crucial to working your way to a muscle up. If 4 archer pull ups are too many to begin with, start with 3 on each arm.

9. Sternum pull ups

This move diverts the focus away from the latissimus dorsi, but it is another important step in the progression towards a muscle up. Do a pull up until the bar is at chest level. Be sure your elbows remain close to your body all through the later part of the move, and that they drive back past your shoulders. This move is not to be mistook for the 'gironda sternum pull up', through which your back is arched.

10. Belly button pull ups

Similar as above, but pull more forcefully until your belly button is at the same level with the bar. Once more, your elbows should brush past your sides, and drive back past your shoulders.

11. One arm towel-assisted pull ups

The lower your hold is on the towel, the less support your other arm will actually make available. Also attempt modifying your grip on the towel to lessen the assistance (hold with only 2 fingers for example). Only go up to 6 reps on each arm, interchanging each arm, rather than the 8 reps the basic routine calls for.

12. One arm towel-assisted pull ups and eccentrics

Release the towel once your chin clears the bar, and lower yourself over a count of 5 seconds. Only go up to 6 reps on each arm, interchanging each arm, rather than the 8 reps the basic routine calls for.

13. Half one arm pull ups (top half)

Begin in mid-range, and pull yourself up through half the range of motion, till your chin clears the bar. Then lower yourself back to mid-range (elbows bent at 90 degrees).

14. One arm pull ups

Pull yourself up through the entire range of motion from a dead end.

4. Kip Up

In the kip up, you lay on your back and produce sufficient force with your lower body (along with some aid from your hands) to blast upward and land on your feet. You will require wrist flexibility, healthy joints, and core strength for this to be accomplished, and a well-padded surface to practice on.

CALISTHENICS

There are three basic components of the kip up. You should practice each one in separate drills before stringing them all together:

- Place your palms on the ground and roll your hips up quickly. Your knees will be just inches from your forehead. This gives you room to be able to accelerate the explosive motion.
- Push your legs upward with explosive power. Your hips should rise even higher, and your lower back should leave the ground, too. This gives you a feel for how much force you must create to achieve a kip up, and helps you learn the motor pattern.
- Land safely on your feet and stand up from there. Only the balls of your feet should touch the ground, and there should be a straight line from your knees to your chest.

Before trying to get your whole body momentarily airborne, practice landing in a bridge after pushing your legs upward. This is how you land in the actual movement, but you will use momentum to help you stand up.

It can be frustrating to learn the kip up, but you must persist and experiment with it. Don't be afraid to mess up or even devise alternatives that work better for you. The payoff is great, and you'll be able to get up strong when life knocks you down.

5. Pistol Squats

Phase One

Start by sitting on a bench with one foot flat on the ground and the other stretched out in front of you. Stretch forward your arms and at the same time press your foot into the ground while tightening your abs. Don't let your heel leave the ground. If you have adequate strength, you should be able to lift yourself off the bench. Once you attain a standing position, try to gradually lower yourself and repeat. You will probably lose control during the lowering phase and wind up plopping down onto the bench at the bottom. That's okay for now. With time your control will improve to the point where you no longer need to sit on the bench.

Phase Two

Stand on a bench with one foot hanging off the edge. Squat down so that the opposite leg drops below the level of the bench. Be certain you stick out your hips and butt, and slightly lean forward. If you are having a hard time attaining stability, hold onto something to support you. A broom handle works well if you are doing these at home. If you have a training companion, have them help you by either holding your hand or standing near you so you can hold them if you lose your balance.

Phase Three

Go down into a deep squat with your two feet flat on the ground. Try to reach one leg out in front of you while balancing on the other. You're presently at the bottom position of a pistol squat. Get at ease with your balance here; it will come easier to some than to others. The moment you can balance in the bottom position, try to stand up. It's fine to use support until you can perform the move self-reliantly. With practice, you will build the required strength and stability to perform the pistol with confidence - then you can move onto advanced pistol squats!

Muscles Used: These squats work similar primary muscle groups used for running, including the hips, hamstrings, quadriceps, gluteus maximus and calves. Hamstrings are found at the back of the upper leg and quadriceps are in the front part of the upper leg. Gluteus maximus muscles, also called buttocks muscles, attach to your hamstrings from above. Calves consist of the soleus and the gastrocnemius muscles and are found at the back of your lower legs. Supportive muscles used during one-legged squats include the upper and lower abdominals and biceps.

6. Handstand Push Ups

This guide focuses at developing the handstand push up against the wall. The first step is to clearly throw yourself up against the wall into a handstand. If this is already too great a step, try beginning with the headstand until you feel at ease upside-down.

You should be capacitated to hold this handstand position against the wall for a minimum of 15 seconds before you start working toward the push up.

When you can hold the static handstand position for enough time, throw a pillow on the ground between your hands. You'll now want to *gradually* lower yourself to the ground. Please don't dive head first through your floor! When you reach the ground put your feet down, then kick back up into a handstand and repeat.

These negative repetitions will help to build the essential pressing strength. In course of these negative reps, you can work on *stopping* yourself in various positions along the way, as well as pushing back up only a couple inches, instead of the whole way.

So to outline, the three methods for building push up strength:

- Lower down slowly.
- Halt and hold yourself at various points.
- Attempt pushing up short distances.

Keeping the replications low and assigning a couple minutes of rest in between your sets will help to develop your shoulder strength. You may choose to work this training into your schedule differently though. With practice, you'll get enough strength to lower down completely to the ground and press back up. Congratulations, there's a handstand push up.

Progressive Exercises:

If you're looking for an exercise apart from handstand push up negatives, there are numerous others that can help you build up your shoulder strength. Nothing too revolutionary, just alternative ways of working out your arms and shoulders.

The first exercise is simply to start lifting your feet in the push up position. You can begin by lifting your feet with a chair, and work your way up to a desk or something higher. The higher your feet, the more stress on your shoulders.

It's also suggested attempting push-ups with your hands by your sides, leaning forward over your hands. You will experience that this places a great deal of stress on the triceps and shoulders. This is also an excellent push up variation to help your planche. You can work on lifting your feet for this exercise as well.

The last exercise is often called a "tiger push up". Begin with your heels against the wall, then go down with your hands and put them on the ground a couple feet in front of your feet. You should look like an opposite "V".

You'll notice that your upper body is in a position to work the shoulders. You can now do push-ups in this position, which will work your shoulders but apply less stress on them than full-on handstand push-ups. Work to raise the feet in this exercise as well to add more bodyweight to the press and intensify difficulty.

7. Dragon Flags

The dragon flag made famous by Bruce Lee is among the three best abdominal exercises that you can do (the other two being the full hanging leg raise and the abs wheel roll out). This exercise can solely build amazingly strong and defined abs as well as great overall core strength so it is a must do exercise for anyone wanting a mastery of the most difficult bodyweight exercises, said that, it should only be attempted by people who have trained for some time and already own a good degree of overall body strength as it has a high risk injury factor if you attempt it before you are ready.

Method of progression: The first stage of progression is to lay with your back flat against a bench, your arms placed behind your head and your hands grasping the edge of the bench. Thereafter, bring your knees in to your waist so that your thighs are at 90 degrees and in one synchronized effort pull up with your hands keeping your whole body rigid until it rises up and your torso points directly towards the ceiling. Once there, remain in that position for a second or two and then lower your body back down under control until your buttocks are just a couple of inches from the bench.

Note, as your body rises to begin the rep, gradually exhale and keep your whole body tensed, as you begin to descend again, gradually inhale with the abdomen and repeat the sequence.

If you notice that even with your legs bent you cannot lift yourself off the bench under control you can simply do partial negatives by lowering yourself from the end of the movement until you reach as low as you can securely go and then pulling your body back up.

The next phase of progression is to gradually extend the legs over a period of time as you get stronger until you can finally do the dragon flag with your legs completely straight.

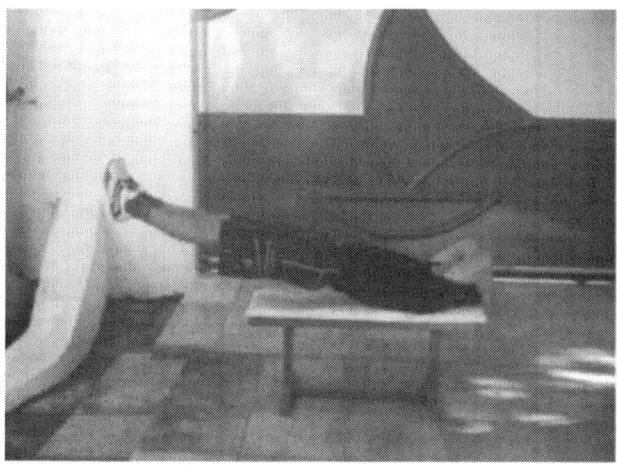

Advice:

- Be sure your shoulders and head are in contact with the bench at all times.
- Pointing your toes helps to keep your body properly aligned.
- Proper muscular coordination is essential to do the dragon flag so a good tool is to stand in front of a mirror and practice tensing as many muscles as possible simultaneously.

8. Jump Muscle Ups

Simply skip the pull-up phase by jumping and either catch above the rings or in support. The main point of this is to get a practical feel for the technique that is required without any real effort on your behalf. If you catch in support be careful to control the jump as too much slack from a big jump coming down on locked out elbows can be dangerous. If you plan on catching in the 'dipped' position be sure your shoulders are ready for the stretch.

CALISTHENICS

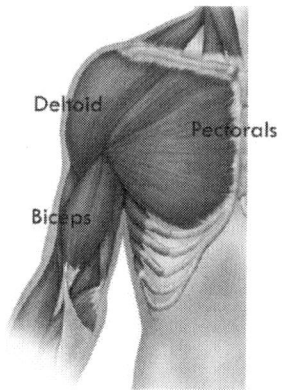 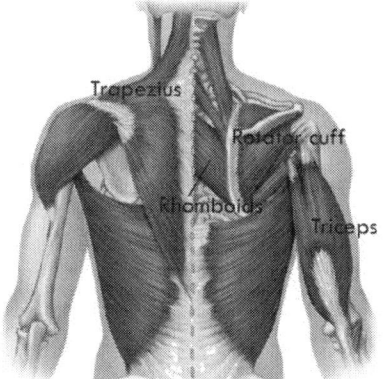

9. Handstands

The handstand is effortlessly one of the most impressive strength feats out there. There's only one feat that is better than handstand – The One-Arm Handstand.

Handstand can be different. There are several alterations of it.; for example, straddle, tuck, pike and regular version. However, form is the most important. Handstand can be straight and arched. Straight is tougher. It needs good shoulder flexibility, hand strength and core strength. But it's stress-free to learn one-arm handstand from straight version rather than from arched.

In accordance to some sources, it's not quite possible to learn "one-armer" from arched or "banana" handstand. Therefore it's better to learn straight version at initial stage. Nonetheless, you might not be able to learn it right away because it is too demanding (especially if your bodyweight is 80 kg and more and you lack shoulder and hip flexibility). Don't get discouraged. Learn arched version first, thereafter, learn the straight one. Learning straight version is concerned with understanding hollow body position. It would be a great idea to allocate some time learning and researching this position to do it perfectly while standing on your hands. Furthermore, you need to work on your shoulder mobility and flexibility big time. That's much more difficult than it sounds. Lack of flexibility may be the single most important problem you need to fix in quest for straight handstand.

Here are the **10 Top Tips**:
1. Push through fingers. We can't stress more on this. The key to holding a handstand is pushing through your fingers. Below are two photos:

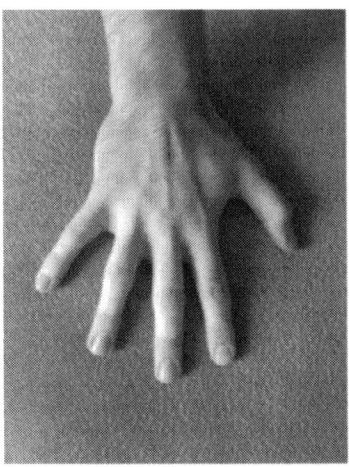

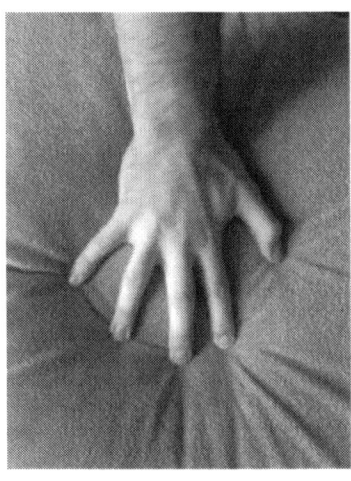

First one – no finger pressure, second – finger pressure. You should always use this method while holding a handstand. Once more, this is the crucial to finding a balance.

2. Work on handstand push-ups. I've seen marvellous help in training free-standing handstand from full range of motion handstand push-ups. You'll develop required strength in shoulders and triceps with this dynamic movement. So you can emphasize on balance more.

3. You need to discover that "sweet spot". You'll quickly find out that you can hold a free-standing handstand for couple of seconds with ease when you find that position where the centre of mass is roughly above your knuckles.

4. Use spotter when possible. The rapid way to learn free-standing handstand is to practice it with spotter. He or she should give the right quantity of support for you not to fall out of balance. This is perhaps the most beneficial way to practice handstand as you learn proper position from the start.

5. Practice kick-ups. It can be stress-free for you to hold a handstand, but you might not be able to kick-up in it all the time. No big deal. Work on kick-ups. Kick up, hold it for a second or two, and then repeat.

6. Use high-frequency. Handstand training entails a lot of repetition. So it would be good idea to practice it on a daily basis. But not to failure. And if you feel that you just can't hold it today no matter what you do, then, it's definitely time for some rest. With practice you'll discover when it's time to train handstand and when it's better to rest. And, of course, with increasing intensity or volume you'll need to slightly cut frequency.

7. Don't skip steps in progression. It will be tempting to hold a free-standing handstand immediately, some "coaches" will tell you to do that. But that's not right. Principles of progressive resistance work here as well. You need to hold wall-supported handstand for at least several sets of 30 sec before moving to next intermediate step – wall-spotted handstand. Then work to sets of at least 20 sec of that. Thereafter you may play with free-standing form. That's just rudimentary progression. Some individuals will need more steps, some - less.

8. Work on both wall-assisted handstand versions. It is important to work on back-to-wall and front-to-wall handstands as well. They both have their advantages and disadvantages and perfectly com-

plement each other.

9. Overcome the fear of falling. There will be anxiety of falling first couple of times. Don't fear, you *will* fall. You will fall several times if you're into this hand balancing thing. It's part of the development. Of course, learn some ways to get out of handstand if something goes off beam. This will add some self-assurance to you. But the best and quickest way to combat fear of falling is just to do that damn handstand over and over. Until you have the confidence. And again spotter will be of use in this situation.

10. Practice more. There's nothing better than practice for acquiring a skill. So practice, practice, practice and then practice some more.

10. 90 Degree Push Up

When you've mastered the floor push-up and the pike push-up, you may want to move onto something even more challenging that can help you train for the mother of all push-ups: handstand push-ups. To get there, start with the 90 degree push-up, in which your feet are elevated to create a 90-degree angle between your upper and lower body. Any typical push-up requires a good deal of shoulder strength, but the 90 degree push-up entails more than most.

Step 1: Place a bench, high chair, wooden box or another kind of solid object with a flat surface on the floor, leaving at least 4 feet of open space on all sides. The bench should be roughly half your height. If you fall, you'll want plenty of room so that you won't land on something or knock over the bench and possibly sustain a serious injury.

Step 2: Stand with your body facing away from the bench, placing yourself about 3 feet from the bench.

Step 3: Place your hands flat on the floor about shoulder-width apart.

Step 4: Place your feet on the bench, and then walk your feet and hands backward to position your trunk perpendicular to the floor, with your hips above your head, your head between your hands and your legs at approximately a 90-degree angle from your trunk. It may help to have a friend look at your position and ensure your body is at an approximately 90-degree angle.

Step 5: Keep your knees stretched and your toes pressing into the bench. Push into your hands to straighten your trunk.

Step 6: Lower your head gradually, making sure you stay in control of your body, until your head touches the floor or your hair scratches it. Work to point your elbows in toward the bench slightly, instead of flaring them out to the sides. If you flare them out, the exercise becomes more of a military press. That's still a good workout for your shoulders, but it won't do much to help you practice the stability you'll need to perform a full handstand push-up.

Step 7: Press into the floor with your hands and then use the strength of your shoulders and core to move back to the starting position. If you can perform another repetition safely, do so; the goal is to be able to repeat the entire move 8 to 12 times.

Things Needed: Bench or chair

Tip: Don't try this exercise if you haven't mastered performing sets of at least 10 to 20 standard, on-the-floor push-ups. Not having the upper body strength required for this exercise is likely to result in serious injury. If you need another type of progression between the 90 degree push-up and the standard push-up, try pikes on the floor. Start with your legs on the floor in a 90-degree pike position, similar to the "downward dog" in yoga. Then lower your body until your forehead nearly touches the floor and push back up to the starting position.

Warning: Whatever type of bench or support you use, make sure it's stable and weighs a significant amount; lightweight chairs will be more likely to tip over when you start moving around, which also can lead to serious injury.

Muscles Used: This exercise also aims at the muscles of the chest, arms, and shoulders, support needed from other muscles results in a wider range of muscles integrated into the exercise. This includes; abdominals, deltoid, pectoralis, triceps brachii.

Below is a diagram to illustrate a progression of pushups.

CALISTHENICS

So this has introduced you to the intermediate calisthenics exercises. Of course, there are many more, but now we will move onto the more advanced moves.

10 ADVANCED EXERCISES

When you are ready to move onto more advanced calisthenics exercises, here is a selection for you to try:

1. One Handed Superman Push Up

Set up: Adopt the push up position with feet shoulder width apart.

Action: Descend into the bottom of the push up. As you rise to the top of the movement, lift out your right arm in front of your body, while lifting your left leg off the floor at the same time so it's in a straight line with your right arm. Pause at the top position for one second. That's one rep. Drop back into the push up and replicate the same action on the other side.

Tips:

- Do not let your torso to rotate at the top.
- Keep your torso straight all through the movement. Do not let your hips or head to sag toward the floor at any point.
- Keep your legs straight through this movement and do not let your knees to bend.

Muscles Worked:

While the push-up principally targets the muscles of the chest, arms, and shoulders, support needed from other muscles results in a wider range of muscles assimilated into the exercise. This includes; abdominals, deltoid, pectoralis, triceps brachii.

2. 2 Finger Push Ups

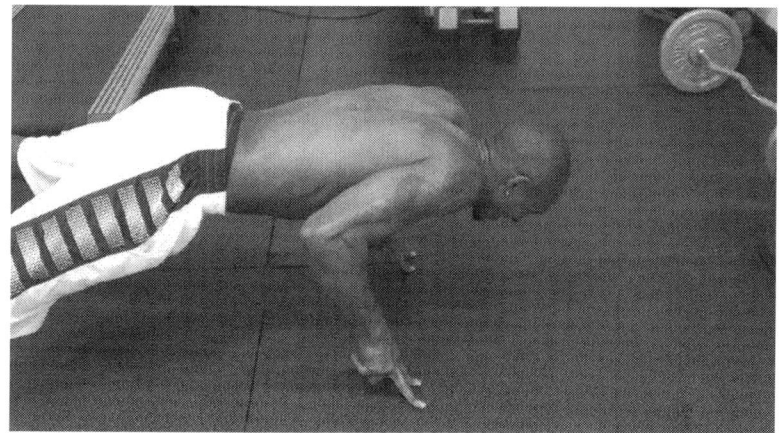

Since Bruce Lee publicly demonstrated two-finger push-ups in 1964, others have attempted to emulate the feat, which requires abundant willpower and strength. But no matter how big a Lee fan you may be, the two-finger push up is not suggested for beginners. If you haven't done anything more exotic than a standard push up, work your way through some basic steps before you try to amaze your friends with your push up expertise.

Step 1: Stretch out face down on the floor or a workout mat. Stretch your legs and spread them as wide as you comfortably can.

Step 2: Place one arm palm-down on the floor, underneath your shoulder or slightly to the outside. Assume a three-point position, balancing yourself on your toes and hand. Place your other hand behind your back and keep your body as straight as possible. Do push-ups with one arm, breathing out as you rise and breathing in when you lower yourself to the floor.

Step 3: Adopt the same position as a one-arm push up, but balance on your fingertips in place of a flat palm. When you succeed at five-fingertip push-ups, do push-ups by gradually removing fingers from the floor, starting with your pinkie, then your ring finger, and subsequently the middle finger.

Step 4: Perform two-finger push-ups with only your thumb and index finger on the floor, spread wide, with the upper joint of both fingers flat on the floor. Place your middle finger beside your index finger – but off the floor – to give your index finger added support.

Tip: An alternative way to build finger strength and work your way up to two-finger push-ups is to start with standard two-arm push-ups, then advance to two-arm fingertip push-ups, then start removing fingers until you're performing two-arm, two-finger push-ups. From there, proceed to one-arm push-ups on two fingers. It can take several months of work before you are capable of performing two-finger push-ups.

Muscles Used: You can alternate fingertip and regular push-ups to gain more benefits for particular muscles. To give your chest a more extensive workout, position your hands wider than shoulder-width apart. To work your triceps more vigorously, put your hands closer together, with the tips of your thumb and first finger touching to form a triangle. Put your feet on a stair or a ledge and execute the push-up to work your shoulders harder. To emphasize on strengthening your wrists, do knuckle push-ups instead, keeping your wrist beneath your elbow. As your fingers, hands and wrists get stronger, try doing push-ups with fewer fingers touching the ground.

3. Human Flag

The human flag is debatably the most visually impressive bodyweight feat of strength anyone's eyes come up with. Any time someone performs a human flag, it unavoidably attracts attention. It takes substantial strength and lots of practice to do the human flag. You have to be very strong, but you also must work specifically towards this skill.

Before embarking on the long, slow journey which is human flag training, be mindful that like all bodyweight exercises, a high strength to mass ratio is vital to performing a human flag. When it comes to the flag, you're only as strong as you are lean, so you shouldn't try to gain weight if you want to excel this move. That said, you can absolutely still develop strength through human flag training.

The best way to practice the human flag is to use a strong vertical pole that's approximately an inch in diameter (thicker poles will pose more of a difficulty). The top hand is typically placed in an overhand grip while the bottom hand is supinated. Grip the pole tight and try to keep both arms as straight as possible.

The main muscles involved in this move are the delts, lats, and oblique. You'll need a good base of strength from exercises like pull-ups and handstand push-ups (or barbell presses) to begin training the flag. Your bottom arm is going to be pressed into the pole to support your outstretched body while your top arm will be pulling you up. On the other hand, both your lats and delts on both sides must engage to accomplish this.

The extreme balance required for this move demands synchronicity between antagonist muscle groups. Once your base is solid with pull-ups and presses, you can get stronger through building up to the full human flag by gradual progression.

The answer is to practice similar positions where you'll have better leverage. Make sure to evenly train both sides.

The Vertical Flag:

Part of what makes the full human flag so difficult is that you're using a comparatively short lever (your arm) to hold up a much longer object (your body). Since you can't make your arms any longer, you need to device ways to make your body shorter to make the flag more practicable.

Begin by trying a variation with your body closer to being vertical than horizontal (with your feet high in the air), almost like a crooked handstand (handstands, by the way, are a great way to complement your human flag training).

Aside from being easier on your arms, this puts less stress on the obliques, lower back, and abdominal muscles, letting you to get a feel for having your body up in the air while you build up the strength to fully stretch your legs horizontally.

Top Down:

Once you can achieve the vertical flag, practice towards lowering your hips down with your legs still up. From here you can advance to putting out one leg, and over time, both legs.

Practicing with your knees bent or your legs in a straddle stance also works well as a pathway to attaining the full human flag. Recall, the closer your legs and torso are to the pole, the better your leverage will be.

Any adjustment that gives you better leverage is a good way to work towards this technique. The important thing is constant practice. As a rule, work up to a minimum of ten-second hold on the easier variations before moving onto more difficult ones.

Bottoms Up:

The moment you can hold a full human flag for a few seconds, you can start trying to get in position from the bottom up. Pressing into the flag is a harder task than lowering from the vertical position. It's like the difference between stopping half way down on a negative one arm push-up, and pressing yourself to that position from the ground.

Tips:

- Feel free to get imaginative with your flag training. Any sturdy surface that permits you to get a good grip with your arms far enough apart is fair game.
- Different objects will pose their own unique challenges. Exercising and strengthening your body is serious business, but it can still be a

lot of fun!

Thus how long will it take to learn to perform a human flag? While it's normal to ask this question, it's suggested that you approach the flag with restraint and patience - don't think about the end result. It's a long journey to get to the human flag and those who go in imagining a quick fix will likely be disappointed.

It takes a lot of practice – even if you are fit already. On the other hand, if you emphasize on the process rather than the result, you'll find it a more profiting experience.

That said, some people can get a brief hold after just a few weeks of practicing, others can take much longer to get off the ground for even a second. It varies for everyone, but if you put in the work, in due course your time will come.

4. One Handed Handstand

The one-handed handstand is a feat of strength, swiftness and balance. Your body is upside down in a vertical stance, as in a normal handstand, but you have just one hand in contact with the ground. Many people relate this style of gymnastics with circus acts or street entertainers. You don't have to be a participant of Cirque du Soleil to perform a one-handed handstand. Nonetheless, it will take a lot of practice and patience to perfect this feat.

Step 1: Practice a regular handstand prior to attempting the one-handed version. You should be able to hold a regular handstand effortlessly for at least 30 seconds before moving to this advanced handstand.

Step 2: Kick into the handstand. Stand with your dominant leg a step behind your non-dominant leg. Lift your arms straight in the air. Put your hands on the floor and propel your feet into the air. Your back leg and arms should move at a similar speed. This is a forceful, quick motion.

Muscles Worked:

A long list of muscles are strengthened while holding a handstand position. Your shoulders, back, arms and chest muscles carry most of your weight while you are upside down, but your whole body must be much tensed while stretching your toes toward the ceiling. The main shoulder and chest muscles utilized in a handstand are your anterior and medial deltoid, and your pectoralis major and minor. The main muscles of your back involved are as follows: serratus anterior, erector spinae, trapezius, latissimus dorsi and quadratus lumborum. Active muscles of your arms are triceps brachii and coracobrachialis. Major muscles of your abdomen are transversus abdominis, rectus abdominis and obliquus externus. All your four quadriceps muscles, inner thigh, hamstrings, buttocks, calf, foot, forearm, hand and neck muscles must be squeezed very tight or you will fall over.

5. Manna

The manna progression is additional of the gymnastic-based exercises within calisthenics. There is no other exercise progression which requires so much stability and core strength to be developed. Body flexibility is also a vital part of the progression as the achievement of the final exercise requires you to display a body position which may appear completely impossible.

Step 1 – Foot Supported L Sit

This can be performed either on the floor or with the use of some elevated bars. Lift your backside off the ground with your hands. Stretch your feet straight out in front of you and utilize them to help assist you in this position. Try to emphasize on extending your scapulae towards the floor.

Step 2 – Advanced Tuck L Sit

The second phase of the manna progression includes the same hand position. The modification is your leg position. This time bend your legs until they are tucked with your feet around a foot and a half from your hands. For your first few stabs you may want to attempt the exercise with your feet assisting your weight on the floor, but before moving to the following step make efforts and be able to balance on your hands with your feet raised.

Step 3 – Straddle L Sit

Balance on your hands using the floor or elevated bars again and spread your legs either side of your arms and extend them out in front of you. By the end of this you will be familiar with the sensation of balancing on your hands only.

Step 4 – V Sit

There are 2 positions to assume in this exercise. The goal here is to strengthen your core so that you will be capable of holding the final position. Begin by sitting on the floor and extending your legs together in the air about a 45 degree angle to the floor. Lean back to keep balance and put your arms out parallel to your legs. Holding this position will strain your core muscles and give you great core balance. From this you should try holding the position while balancing on your hands. This is the best training for the manna exercise.

You may be fascinated to see some V sit eccentrics if you find this exercise difficult.

Step 5 – Manna

The final step of this progression. Balance on your hands and bring your legs together in front of you in an L sit posture. Start bringing your legs up until you are in the V sit and begin going further until your back is nearly parallel with the floor and your shins are almost touching your face. This is an awesome progression in strength, flexibility, mobility and balance.

CALISTHENICS

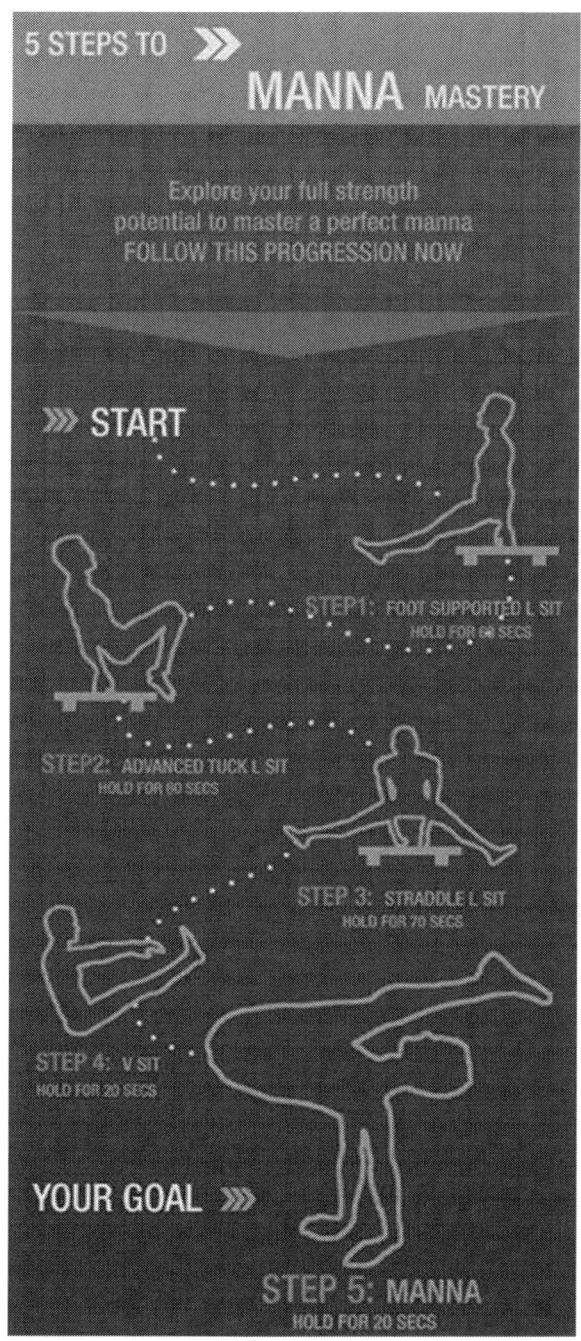

Muscles Used: This exercise is a full body workout. It targets legs, arms, core, etc.

6. Planche

The planche is an important gymnastics technique in which the body is held parallel to the ground, reinforced only by the hands and arms (with the feet raised). This needs an incredible amount of strength and balance.

You will frequently see the planche featured in competitive gymnastics but it's also a common exercise for recreational athletes in bodyweight and calisthenics movements.

The body positioning for the planche is outlined in below:

Hands

Hand posture is down to personal preference. Here are the common distinctions:

- Fingers forward
- Fingers on the side
- Fingertips hold
- Flat hand

Practice with your hands positioning and find the grip that works best for you.

Arms

Arms should be stretched, with the elbows locked out.

Torso

Muscles engaged forming a straight line down the body, parallel to the ground.

Hips and legs

Hold the hips level with the shoulders. Bring the legs close together for a complete planche.

Unless you're a skilled gymnast or have been training devotedly for the planche skills it's improbable that you're going to be able to perform the hold immediately. You need to work through the planche progressions to build up the needed strength and skills.

It's vital that you approach planche training with the proper mind set else you're destined for frustration. Learning the planche is characteristically not a quick process and in most cases you're looking to at least of 6 months training, but this differs considerably depending on the person in question and their current abilities, and can often take longer.

As with most progressive bodyweight exercises the two most important facets of your training are patience and commitment. Improvements will come steadily, but incrementally.

Planche progressions

There are four major progression exercises recommended for the planche, these are; the frog stand, tuck planche, advanced tuck planche, straddle planche and finally onto the full planche.

Training notes

- Hold each progression for as long as you are at ease and in good form.
- Combine each set until you have 60 seconds of total hold time (however many sets this may take!).
- Have a mastery of each progression before moving onto the next

(60 second consecutive hold) and repeat the process.

Planche progression exercises:

The progressions below are adopting a base level of fitness and you should have a solid physical base through planks, push-ups, pull-ups and dips before delving into the progressions.

Frog stand - This is the starting point of planche training. Adopt a full squat position and place your hands on the ground, in front of the feet. Your knees should be resting against the elbows for support. Lean forward, taking weight onto the hands. With practice you will be able to remove the feet totally from the ground. Practice this position until you hit your 60 second hold time prior to moving to the next progressing as described in the training notes above.

Tuck planche - A comparable position to the frog stand except the knees are pressed into the chest so your straight arms are totally supporting your body weight. Practice constantly, targeting at lift your hips to shoulder height. Progress to the advanced tuck planche when you can sustain the standard hold for 60 seconds with raised hips and straight arms.

Advanced tuck planche - The main modification with the advanced tuck planche is back positioning. The advanced tuck planche is practiced with a straight back whereas the standard tuck planche is performed with a curved back. Extend the hips up and behind you until the back straightens out and move one when you can withstand the straight back hold for 60 seconds.

Straddle planche - The straddle planche improves on the tuck planche position by extending the legs out, held straight from the body. When in the tuck planche position, gradually move the legs out from the chest behind you (you will need to learn forward to counter balance the shift in weight). The wider the legs the easier it is to balance, struggle to bring the legs closer together as you advance. Target for ten second holds with the straddle planche due to the increased difficulty.

Once you've fully had a mastery of the static strength planche you can start training for some dynamic movement to the exercise and introduce planche push-ups for additional intensity.

Planche tips:

- Try to hold the hips level with the shoulders.

- Make sure elbows are straight (bent arm planches will deter progress by lessening the intensity).

- Be constant. Train the static progression holds every day for maximum effect.

- Be patient. Make small, incremental progress.

- With each workout, endeavour to increase position hold time or the extension of the position.

- Even minute changes in body position can extremely increase the difficulty of the exercise.

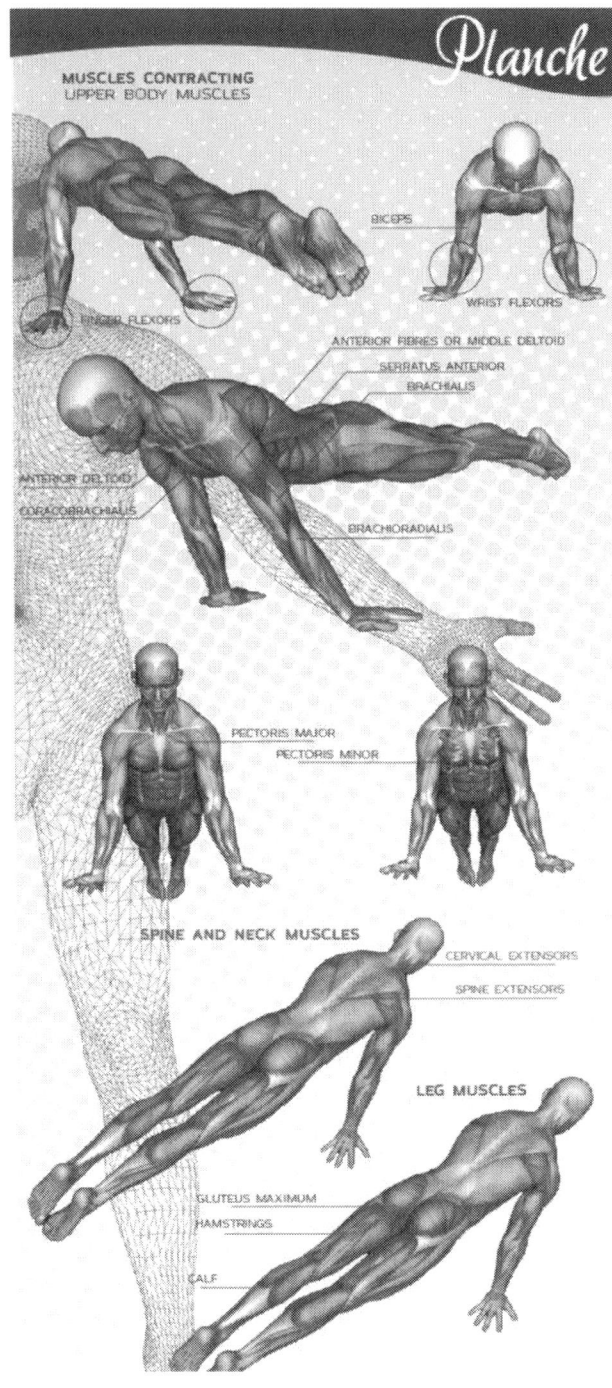

7. Levers

Attaining a front lever entails serious back strength as well as total body control. These are the varieties accessible to you.

Tuck Front Lever

The simplest variation on the front lever is the tuck front lever. Suspend from a pull-up bar and squeeze your legs into your chest while rolling your hips back until your torso is parallel to the ground. Try staying up and hold this position for as long as you can.

More improved variations can include extending one leg while keeping the other tucked or keeping both legs in a half-tuck position. There are many steps in between the tuck front lever and the full position.

Straddle Front Lever

By opening your legs in a course of a front lever, you're not only changing the balance, you're also shortening the lever, both of which make this move a little easier than a full front lever (though still harder than the tuck lever). You'll need better than average hip mobility to pull off a good straddle front lever, so make sure you're stretching frequently.

Front Levers for Reps

When building up to a front lever hold, doing front levers for reps can be a very beneficial tool. Keep your entire body tight as you use your lats to pull your body into the lever stance, then lower back down to a dead hang and repeat. The movement pattern is alike to a dumbbell pullover, apart from you're moving your entire body instead of only a dumbbell!

When your form breaks down, switch to suspending leg raises. This can make for a very challenging superset.

Front Lever to Muscle-up

The front lever to muscle-up is an excellent way to work towards improving your front lever hold, as well as a complex move in its own right. It's simpler to do the muscle-up first, then lower yourself into the lever, keeping total body tension the whole time. Hold the lever position, then pull yourself back over the bar and repeat. Try using a false grip for this exercise.

Practice, Practice, Practice

Working your way up to a front lever hold can take an extremely long time. Be patient and slowly build to several seconds on each step prior to moving onto the next one. If you discover yourself getting stagnant in your development, take a break from front lever training while you continue to work the fundamentals (pull-ups, push-ups, etc.) then come back to it after a few weeks. In the big picture, a little time off can sometimes give you a new focus.

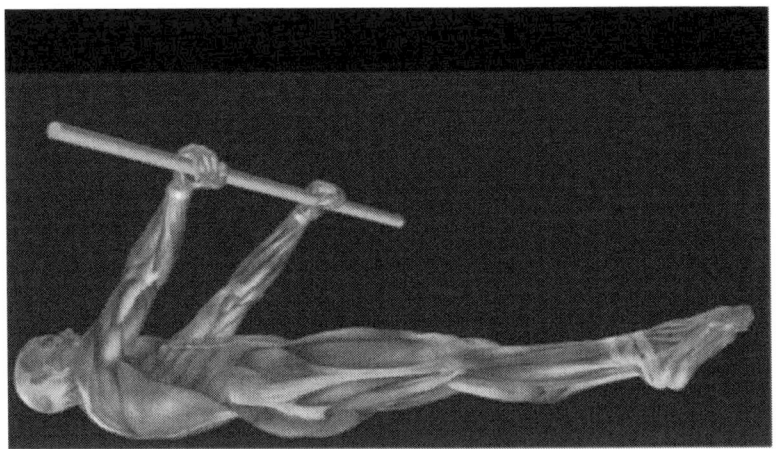

8. Typewriter Pull Ups

This move will upsurge the challenge to your muscles in a number of ways. Each rep, comprising of a shift to both sides, will take longer than a characteristic pull-up, and also place more tension on the muscles when maintaining the top position.

Begin in a pull-up position with your palms facing away from you, shoulder-width apart. Go to the top normally with your chin even with the bar. In a controlled manner, move your body to the left so that your chin is even with the back of your left hand. This posture will overwork the left side of your back as you lower into the bottom position. Return to the middle and this time move to the right and lower accordingly. Think of the shift as the move an outdated typewriter makes when it needs to be reset.

Your lats, traps, deltoids, forearms and biceps will be strained to the max when one side or your back must support 90% of your bodyweight during the lowering phase of the rep.

Once you have a mastery of it...

- *Progression I:* Escalate your reps (with perfect form) to six
- *Progression II:* Hold the top position for a full two seconds
- *Progression III:* Extend the lowering phase to last six seconds and include a weight belt.

9. Clapping Pull Ups

The clapping pull up is the thing to do if you want to advance your sporting performance, endurance and upper body strength. Although it is very comparable to the standard exercise, the speed of movement required to rise high above the bar, remove your hands, clap and then place your hands back to their initial position develops amazing explosive power that is well worth earning.

Method:

This exercise entails you to do the complete reverse of what you would usually do for pull ups because unlike the standard version were you perform the exercise slow and under control the secret of this one is speed of movement. To achieve the height necessary to clap in mid air your body needs to move very fast which also eases the building of the explosive power mentioned earlier. However, due to the nature of this workout do not attempt it until you have already mastered the standard exercise and feel you have the coordination and strength needed to attempt it safely.

Before starting always ensure you have warmed up properly and adopt the normal pull up position. From there you need to pull up yourself as fast as you can so that your chin rises well above the bar, rapidly take your hands away, clap and then return them to their original position. Also keep in mind that because of the coordination needed this is an exercise were practice makes perfect so do not be thwarted if it takes you a while to nail it.

Tips:

- Be sure to thrust your chest forward and lean back a little as you start each rep so that your chin is away from the bar.

- Try to practice this exercise on a bar that you can reach on your tip toes so that you do not have to drop far if you get it wrong.

- Recall speed is the key, the faster you move the more chance of success you have.

- Ensure there are no dangerous hindrances in your path in case you drop back to the ground.

- Inhale before the start of each rep and try to imagine your body being as light as possible.

- Exhale the air powerfully as you go upwards (This will help to develop power comparable to that displayed by martial artists when they perform breaking techniques).

10. Muscle Ups

Below is a great **technique for getting your first muscle up**:

No single bodyweight exercise works your entire upper body as scrupulously as a muscle-up. It is truly the king of bodyweight exercises. This guide has been produced for towards accomplishing your first muscle-up on a straight bar.

Before you can achieve a muscle-up on a straight bar, you must be capable of comfortably performing pull-ups and dips, but there is no set rule for how many reps are required as a prerequisite. Some people who can only deal with six or seven pull-ups can do a muscle-up, others who can complete twenty dead hang pull-ups still repeatedly fail at getting through the sticking point; the muscle-up is an exceptional challenge and must be treated as such.

Before you are ready to do a muscle-up, you should rehearse doing pull-ups with an overstated range of motion. Instead of stopping when the bar is under your chin, pull it all the way down past your chest. Get as far over the bar as you can!

It can be beneficial to practice an improved muscle-up on a bar that is about chest height so you can utilize your legs to help jump into it. (If you can't find a low bar, bring a step or a bench up to a high bar.) This will permit you get an experience for the transition from being under the bar to getting on top without having to overcome your full bodyweight. With practice, you'll learn to depend less on your legs and do most of the work with your upper body. Once you've gotten the hang of jumping into a muscle-up, you're ready to try the real one.

When you are learning to do a muscle-up, it's useful to use your hips and legs to produce additional power to get your chest beyond the bar. Do all that it takes to get yourself up and over – nobody's first muscle-up looks flawlessly clean. As you get stronger and more at ease with the movement pattern, you can begin to work cleaning up your muscle-up technique, as well as working on other types of improved muscle-ups.

Similar to all bodyweight exercises, core strength plays a big part in doing a muscle-up. Always rehearse your planks and L-sits to keep your abs strong.

Novices might find it helpful to use a false grip when doing a muscle-up on a bar. This involves bending your wrists over the bar so that your palms are facing toward the ground.

Just like when you are working on getting your first pull-up, it can be useful to rehearse negatives and use manual aid while learning to do a muscle-up. If you are going to spot someone on a muscle-up, I recommend giving them a boost by holding them under one or both heels, as if you were helping them over a fence.

Hopefully now you know how to progress your exercises to suit your ability level – which will increase as you workout. The more you do, the more resources you'll find to assist you.

TOP TRAINING PROGRAMS

Now that you've had a look at – and tried – a lot of calisthenics exercises, it's time to look at workout programs. Here is a selection, designed for different end goals.

Beginner Circuit Workout

Perform 3 cycles. 30 second rest period between exercises, and 3 minute rest period between cycles. There are 8 exercises:

- 10 pull ups
- 10 chin ups
- 20 dips
- 25 jump squats

- 20 push ups
- 50 crunches
- 10 burpees

- 30 second jump rope

Intermediate Circuit Workout

Do 2 cycles, 30 second rest between exercises and 3 minute rest between each cycle. There are 8 exercises.

- 5 muscle ups
- 50 push ups
- 25 jump squats
- 15 burpees
- 15 pull-ups
- 1 minute leg flutters

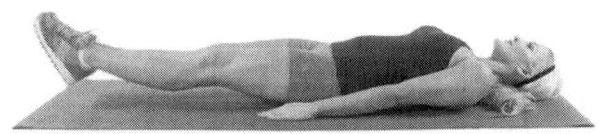

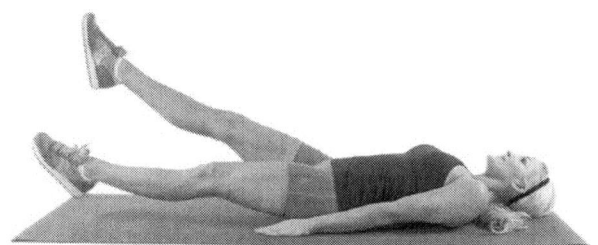

- 10 pull-ups
- 30 second sprint nonstop

Advanced Circuit Workout

Do 1 cycle, no rest between exercises; each exercise is 30 seconds long. There are 10 exercises.

- Hold a handstand for 30 seconds
- Jump squats
- Wall push ups

- Kick up push ups

CALISTHENICS

- Squat position move side to side

- Planks

- Dips
- Jumping lunges

- Single Leg Hops
- Pull-ups

Extreme Circuit Workout

Do 3 cycles, 30 second rest between exercises and no rest between cycles. There will be 8 exercises.

- 10 second back lever hold

- 7 second human flag hold
- 5 second front lever hold
- 15 second bent arm planche hold

- 30 second handstand hold
- 3 very slow muscle ups
- 10 slow dips
- Pull up hold position for 30 seconds

Mass Building Program

Week 1:

Monday

<u>Chest Workout</u>: 4 Sets

- 15 Regular Push-Ups
- 5 Diamond Push-Ups
- 10 Dips
- 10 Arching Push-Ups

- 10 Decline Push-Ups

- 10 Dips on Straight Bar

Rest for 2 minutes then go through all of them again until you finish 4 sets.

After you are done with your Chest then move on to Back exercises below.

<u>Back Workout</u>: 3 Cycles

- 10 Wide Pull-Ups
- 5 Close Grip Pull-Ups
- 5 Wide Grip Behind Neck Pull-Ups

- 5 Shoulder Width Behind Neck Pull-Ups
- 5 Upside Down Pull-Ups

Tuesday

<u>Arms Workout</u>: 5 Sets

- 10 Shoulder Width Chin Ups
- 20 Wide Grip Australian Chin Ups
- 10 Dips
- 20 Bench Dips
- 10 Close Grip Chin Ups
- 20 Close Grip Australian Chin Ups

- 10 Dips on Straight Bar
- 20 Bench Dips

Wednesday

<u>Legs Workout</u>: 5 Cycles

- 10 Pistol Squats on each leg
- 20 Hannibal Squats (by putting your feet together when you squat)

- 15 Pyramid Calf Raises (do 15 calf raises, rest for 2 seconds, then do 14, and so on)
- 20 In & Out Squat Jumps
- 20 Lunge Walks

- 1min Wall Sit

Thursday

<u>Chest Workout</u>: 4 Sets

- 15 Regular Push Ups
- 5 Diamond Push Ups
- 10 Dips
- 10 Arching Push Ups (your hips will be low to the ground and your chest will be up)
- 10 Decline Push Ups
- 10 Dips on Straight Bar

Rest for 2 minutes; then go through all of them again until you finish 4 sets.

<u>Back Work out</u>: 3 Cycles

- 10 Wide Pull Ups
- 5 Close Grip Pull Ups
- 5 Wide Grip Behind Neck Pull Ups
- 5 Shoulder Width Behind Neck Pull Ups
- 5 Upside Down Pull Ups

Friday

<u>Arms Workout</u>: 5 Sets

- 10 Shoulder Width Chin Ups
- 20 Wide Grip Australian Chin Ups
- 10 Dips
- 20 Bench Dips
- 10 Close Grip Chin Ups
- 20 Close Grip Australian Chin Ups
- 10 Dips on Straight Bar
- 20 Bench Dips

Saturday

<u>Legs Workout</u>: 5 Cycles

- 10 Pistol Squats on each leg
- 20 Hannibal Squats
- 15 Pyramid Calf Raises (15, 14, 13…)
- 20 In & Out Squat Jumps
- 20 Lunge Walks
- 1min Wall Sit

Follow the same routine for the rest 3 weeks. Try to decrease your rest time between exercises and sets over the course of 4 weeks.

Weight Loss

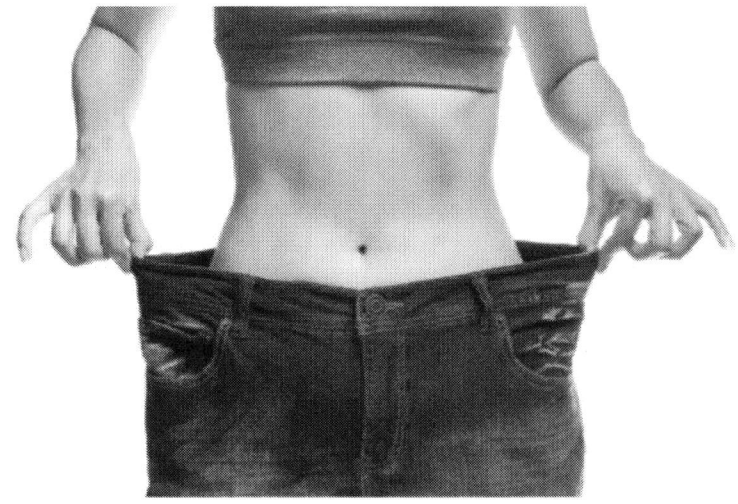

You can choose to repeat each cycle for 30 minutes or 5 sets. Complete each cycle with little to no rest between exercises and rest for 1-2 minutes between sets.

Beginner

- 15 Jumping Jacks
- 10 Squats
- 10 Stationary lunges for each leg
- 5 Knee Push-ups
- 15 Jumping Jacks
- 10 Alternating forward lunges for each leg
- 10 Squats
- 5 Incline push-ups
- 15 Jumping Jacks

Intermediate

- 25 Jumping Jacks

- 20 Squats
- 15 Stationary lunges for each leg
- 10 Incline push-ups
- 25 Jumping Jacks
- 15 Alternating forward lunges for each leg
- 15 Jump Squats
- 5 Push ups
- 25 Jumping Jacks

Advanced

- 50 Jumping Jacks
- 20 Jump Squats
- 10 Jump lunges for each leg
- 15 Push-ups
- 50 Jumping Jacks
- 10 Alternating forward then reverse lunges for each leg
- 20 Jump Squats
- 15 Push ups
- 50 Jumping Jacks

You can make each exercise more difficult by adding a jump to it.

Here are some more options for workout routines.

Lower Body Cardio Routine:

Repeat 4-5 times

Here is a fast and challenging training to build both leg speed and endurance.

- Run or bike 3 minutes

- 20 Squats
- 15 Lunges for each leg
- 25 Calf raises

Upper/Lower Back Balance Cycle:

Repeat 2-3 times

So as to balance out doing several sets of push-ups or other pushing exercises, add in the below exercises for 2-3 sets at the end of the workout to avoid internal rotation of the shoulder girdle.

- 25 Reverse Push Ups

CALISTHENICS

- 25 Birds

- 1 min Plank pose

Push/Pull Upper Body Cycle:

Repeat 4-5 times

To completely work the upper body, balance out the pushing muscles (chest, shoulders and triceps) with the pulling muscles (biceps, forearms, back)

- Push-Ups - max reps
- 20 Reverse Push-Ups
- Pull-Ups - max reps
- 20 Birds
- Abs of choice – 50

Abdominal Cycle:

Perform this 2-3 times in the course of the workout and 4-5 times a week. It is fine to do abdominals and cardio exercises several days a week.

- 25 Crunches
- 25 Reverse Crunches

CALISTHENICS

- 25 Double Crunches

Double Crunch

1. Lay on your back with ankels crossed and hand at your ears. Bend your knees 90 degrees and lower until almost touching the floor.

2. Cruch up by raising your knees to your chest and chest to knees. Lower back to starting postition.

- 25 Left Crunches
- 25 Right Crunches
- 25 Bicycle Crunches

- 1 min Plank pose

6 Month Beginner Plan

Here is a workout plan to help beginners get started:

Month 1

Full Body Routine

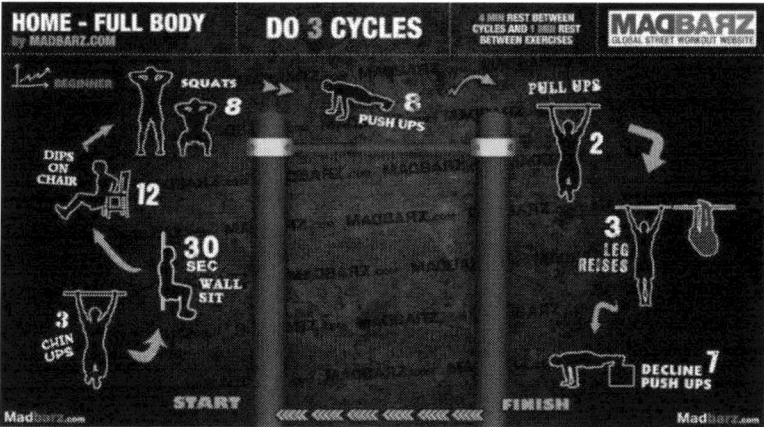

This is to be done *at least* three days a week.

Month 2

Upper Body Routine

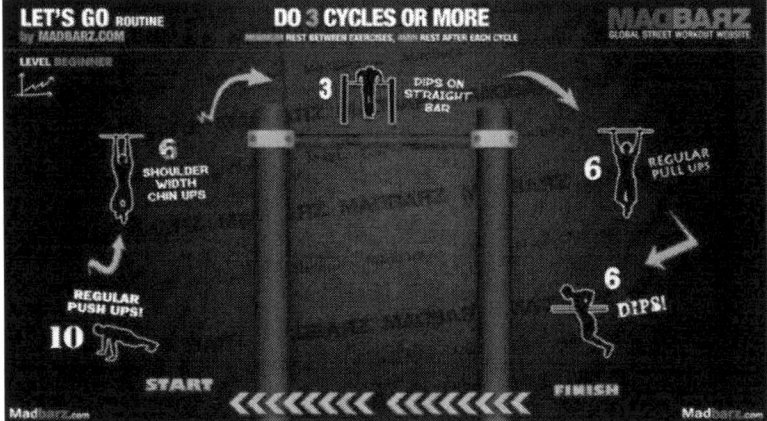

This is also to be done *at least* three days a week.

Month 3

In month 3, complete *both* routines (the Full Body and the Upper Body) shown above for *at least* three days a week. Combine these routines on the same day.

For the last week of this month, work only 50 percentage of your usual load.

Month 4

Muscle Up Hunt

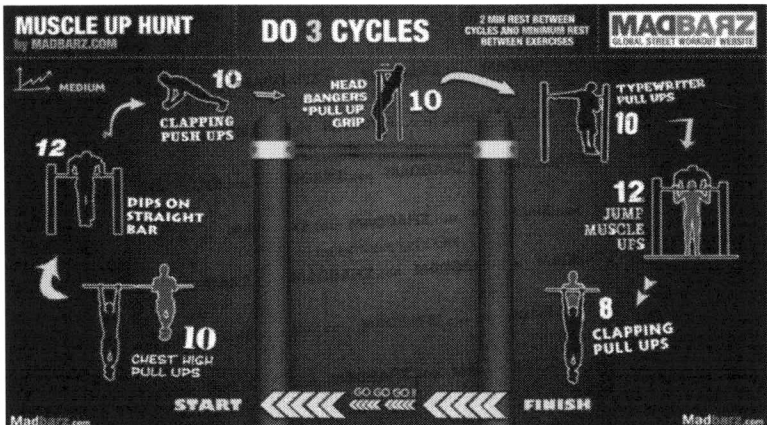

- Monday – Muscle Up Hunt + Full Body Routine
- Wednesday – Upper Body Routine + Full Body Routine
- Friday – Muscle Up Hunt + Full Body Routine

On the additional days do leg dominant routines.

Tip: Always aim for at least 5 reps for each exercise if possible. If you are unable to perform 1 rep of given exercise, then you should regress to an easier progression.

Month 5

For this month, you need to do the **Muscle Up Progression**. This is:

- Explosive pull ups 5 reps
- Explosive pull ups with hand rotation 5 reps
- Jumping into the muscle up and go back into a negative pull up 5 reps

Here is the routine for the month:

- Monday – Muscle Up Progression + Muscle Up Hunt
- Wednesday – Muscle Up Progression + Full Body Routine
- Friday – Muscle Up Progression + Muscle Up Hunt

Add leg routine on additional days.

Month 6

This is the challenge, to see how far you've come.

For more information watch 'Tycho Bar Brothers Groningen Examen' on YouTube.

You have 3 minutes to do the following routine:

- 4 muscle ups
- 15 dips
- 20 push-ups
- 10 jumping squats
- 10 leg raises
- 4 muscle ups

Warm Up Routine

If you are not running to the park or your workout area, it is very important to include a warm-up series before you start your workout of the day. A warm-up circulates blood to the muscles and makes them ready for the vigorous activities to come and should be done for a minimum of 10 minutes before *all* exercise routines you do. Consequently, the following dynamic stretches defined below will help you increase your range of motion, achieve kinesthetic consciousness of the items around you, and be essential to injury prevention.

Light jog

A little bit of cardio is necessary to starting a good warm-up. It is always suggested to take a light jog to your place of exercise. On the other hand, if this isn't an option for you, make sure you jog a minimum of 300 yards (3 football fields) to warm-up. A light jog gets the blood circulating throughout the body so the required materials for performance are accessible to your muscles.

Total Time = 1-2 min

Jumping Jacks

After your light jog, your heart rate should be a little bit elevated and you should have adequate blood supply to the muscles. Jumping jacks are a great dynamic stretch that prepares the lats, shoulders and upper back for the exercise. They should also withstand an elevated heart rate so blood is constantly being delivered to these muscles.

Total Time = 1 min

Arm circle series

Now that you are sweating a little bit and feeling warm, your muscles are prepared to hold back a little stress, but nothing too strenuous. With your arms held out, rotate them forward in small circles. Ensure that your palms are down. Next, swap directions and rotate your arms backwards with your palms up. To conclude, replicate these motions once more but rotating in big circles. Sustain each section of the workout for one minute each.

Total Time = 4 min

Huggers

Time to relax! Fake being Michael Phelps and swing your arms at the same time around your body hugging yourself. Then repel your arms straight away back until they fully extend behind your back. Recall, keep moving!

This should make all the muscles in your chest and upper to mid back prepared for action.

Total Time =1 min

Bent Over Huggers

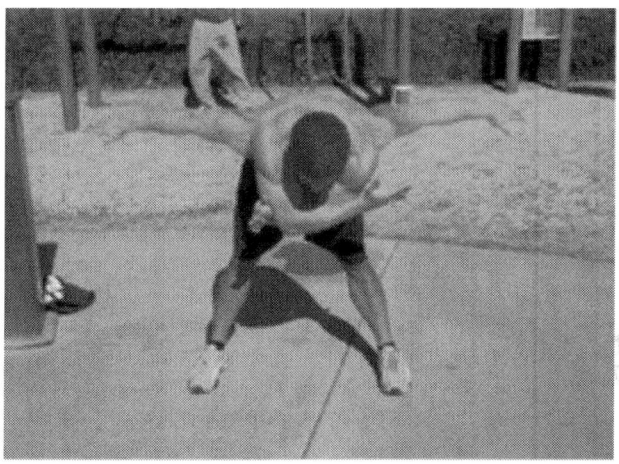

Next, perform the same motion but in a bent over posture with your legs widely spread. This should offer a stretch to the low back and hamstrings while continuing to loosen up your chest and back.

Total Time = 1 min

Dangling Arm Circles

Finally, cool down a little by dangling one of your arms in a bent over posture with your legs wide spread. Then, start rotating that arm clockwise. Carry on this motion for thirty seconds and then swap directions rotating counter-clockwise for an extra thirty seconds. Repeat this with the other arm for another thirty seconds for each direction. With the aid of gravity this dynamic stretch cools you down and circulates blood to the upper extremities.

Total Time = 2 min

Shake it out

Shake it all out and prepare yourself mentally to be pushed. It's time for the workout!

Cool Down Routine

This is a cool down routine that can be done after any type of exercise.

Cool Down Stretches:

- Toe Touch – 30 sec

- Inside Thigh - 30 sec for each side

- Wide Toe Touch – 30 sec

- Standing Quadriceps – 30 sec for each leg

- Hip Flexor and Arm Cross Pull – 30 sec for each side

CALISTHENICS

- Overhead Triceps – 30 sec each hand

- Downward Dog – 30 sec

- Downward Dog – Leg Lift/Hip Openers – 30 sec

- Plank Calf Stretch – 30 sec on each side

- Modified Pigeon – 30 sec on each side

- Cobra – 30 sec

- Child's Pose – 30 sec

- Deep Glute Stretch – 30 sec on each side

- Lying Torso Twist – 30 sec on each side

- Full Body Stretch – 30 sec

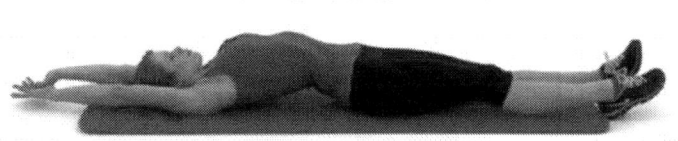

Utilize smooth and skillful motions to go through each one of these movements. You don't want to bounce or force a range of motion that is hurting, as this could end up doing far more harm than good, and even causing injury. As you can, push the range of motion, very gradually and very gently, but never to the point of pain.

LOOKING AT YOUR DIET

When looking at calisthenics, another important area to consider is **your diet**. Getting your eating plan right is very important for gaining and maintaining the physique you desire.

Diet and nutrition are a crucial component to accomplishing your fitness objectives, whatever they might be. A "*diet*" does *not* imply you are going on Atkins or Jenny Craig or others. If you are eating food, you are on a diet. Your diet is just what you are taking into your body. You are a machine; you use energy from what you eat. A diet is to a person as petrol is to your car. Many people give the impression that they are afraid of the word "diet", almost like it's disgraceful. What is shameful - is doing nothing about your situation. If you are weighty right now and you want to get healthy, it's shameful to do nothing about it. If you are overweight and are contented with it, good for you! The shame is not in being overweight, the shame is when you don't want to be overweight and aren't taking any action.

If your fitness goals are to *achieve muscle mass*, there is an excellent chance you are going to need to change your diet to ingest more healthy calories. If your fitness goals are to *lose excessive fat*, you may not need to consume less calories; you just need stop eating junk, start consuming healthy foods, and get physical.

As a machine, you need to take care of yourself. McDonald's five times a week is not taking care of yourself. It is necessary to put in clean healthy nutrients. Let's reason this out for a minute, if you've ever attempted growing any fruits or vegetables, you'll realize that you need to make sure the plant is being provided with the right quantity of nutrients. Excessive and they won't grow, and if they do, they will grow bad and the produce won't be what you had expected. You need to put in the right quantities of the right things to "run" the way you are supposed to.

All this means is that, you can't be consuming greasy foods and highly refined complex carbohydrates into your body: it isn't what your body was intended to run on. In place of eating Bonbon's and Cheerrio's, snack on some Nori Seaweed or an Apple. In place of eating a burger at McDonald's, cook yourself a delicious marinated chicken breast. If you lack time, make the time, where there is a will there is a way. You don't need to consume things you hate, if you do, you most likely won't succeed. All it takes is being committed to yourself, wake up earlier and cook all your meals for the day, or cook your meals for the following day at night.

Your life isn't going to change just because you want it to. It's going to change because you took a decision and made it change. *Nobody* is going to change *your* life for *you*, keep that in mind.

3 Sample Diets For All Needs

You will need to concentrate on what you're eating as much as your exercise. You will need to combine the right workout plan with smart food choices for the best effect.

Lean and Mean Diet Plan

This diet follows four main principles:

- *Principle one*: Cut out junk food.
- *Principle two*: Eat organic.
- *Principle three*: Consume protein, and lots of it!
- *Principle four*: Don't forget grains and dairy.

Cut Out Junk

Due to bad diet, an estimated **70% of all adults in the United States are overweight or obese**, according to the *Centers for Disease Control and Prevention*. This because of all the fat and sugar found in our foods – and that includes a lot of supposed diet foods.

If you want to achieve the right, healthy body you will need to ensure that you read all the labels of everything you eat. You'll want to know exactly what you're putting in your body at times.

Eat Organic

Fruit and vegetables are completely loaded with all sorts of important vitamins and minerals your body needs not only to build quality muscle, but to also control its every function. We can eat as many of these as we want with any diet, because all they do is help us!

These organic items are easy to get hold of, and simple to include in our everyday diet. Hopefully, they are something that you eat a lot of already, so the change won't be too dramatic!

Consume Protein, and lots of it!

It's important to look at where our food is sourced, because a lot of animals are fed unhealthy grains and given antibiotics to cope with their awful living environments, so the end result is something not so pleasant.

Sticking with organic products can help to negate this, because these animals are raised as nature intended.

Don't Forget Grains and Dairy

Eliminating grains and dairy from your diet can have a disadvantageous impact on your health. With this, you merely need to get the balance right.

Eat fresh, eat natural, eat whole, and you're certain to see remarkable results in your fitness and all-around health.

Tip: **Keep a Food Diary**

Keeping a food diary is a great way to keep track of exactly how many calories you are consuming. As long as you are honest – after all, you will only be fooling yourself! This may give you an idea of where you are going wrong (if anywhere) and the visual reminder will help keep you on track.

Muscle Mass Diet Plan

Workout Day Meal Plan

Breakfast (Meal 1)

- 1.5 cups oatmeal (120g), measured uncooked
- 1 cup egg whites
- 2 omega-3 whole eggs
- 1 tbsp all-natural peanut butter

Mid-morning (Meal 2)

- 2 cups low-fat cottage cheese
- 1 cup berry of choice (strawberries, blueberries, raspberries)

Lunch (Meal 3)

- 2 slices Ezekiel 4:9 bread
- 6 oz turkey breast (deli sliced, not packaged)
- Large leaf spinach, unlimited
- half tomato, medium
- Mustard, unlimited
- 1 small sweet potato (150g), measured uncooked

Midday (Meal 4)

<u>Pre-workout</u>

- half of large banana
- 4 small strawberries
- 1 scoop whey isolate protein of choice

<u>Post-workout</u>

- 50g fast-digesting carb (e.g. white baked potato, white rice, instant oatmeal, rice cakes, white bread, bagels, cereals)
- 1.5 scoops whey isolate protein of choice

Dinner (Meal 5)

- 8 oz lean-fat trimmed pork chop
- 1 tbsp organic virgin coconut oil
- 400g acorn squash, measured uncooked
- 340g (usually one steam bag) green veggie of choice (e.g. broccoli, asparagus, green beans, cauliflower)

Evening Snack (Meal 6)

- 8 oz nonfat Oikos Greek yogurt, vanilla or plain
- 1 tbsp all-natural peanut butter
- 1 tbsp sugar-free chocolate syrup
- 10 almonds, crushed

Nutrient Breakdown

- Calories: 3,040
- Carbs: 323g
- Fiber: 60g
- Protein: 271g
- Total Fat: 78g
- Sat. Fat: 28g

Rest Day Meal Plan

Breakfast (Meal 1)

- 1 cup oatmeal (80g), measured uncooked
- 3/4 cup egg whites
- 4 omega-3 whole eggs
- 1 tbsp virgin coconut oil

Mid-morning (Meal 2)

- 2 cups low-fat cottage cheese
- 4 tbsp salsa
- 1 scoop whey protein isolate of choice

Lunch (Meal 3)

- 2 slices Ezekiel 4:9 bread
- 6 oz turkey breast (deli sliced, not packaged)
- Large leaf spinach, unlimited
- Half tomato, medium
- Mustard, unlimited

Midday (Meal 4)

- 2 mozzarella sticks
- 6 oz deli chicken or turkey breast (deli sliced, not packaged), wrapped around cheese

Dinner (Meal 5)

- 8 oz salmon, fillet or packaged
- 1 tbsp extra-virgin olive oil
- 16 oz California Medley Mix, one large frozen bag
- 75g sweet potato, measured uncooked

Evening Snack (Meal 6)

- 10 oz nonfat Oikos Greek yogurt, vanilla or plain
- 1 tbsp all-natural peanut butter

- 1 tbsp sugar-free chocolate syrup
- 10 almonds, crushed

Nutrient Breakdown:
- Calories: 3,000
- Carbs: 210g
- Fiber: 35g
- Protein: 305g total
- Fat: 112g
- Sat: Fat 40g

Female Diet Plan

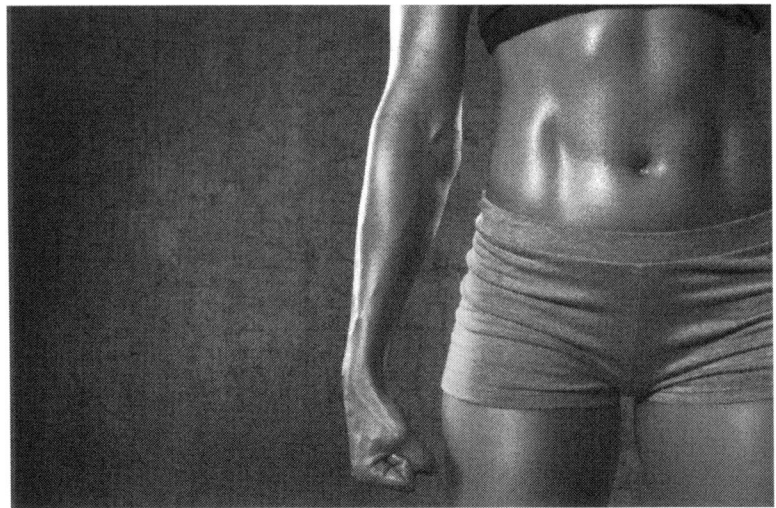

The calorie allowance for men and women is different, which is below is a suitable sample diet for around a 125-pound female:

Breakfast:

- 5 Egg Whites
- Oatmeal 1/2 cup

Morning Snack:

- Protein Shake 1 serving with water
- 1 medium apple

Lunch:

- Lean Meat (poultry, beef, fish, etc.) 4 ounces
- Brown Rice 1/3 cup
- Green Veggies 1 cup

Post-Workout:

- Protein Shake

- Nuts 1 ounce
- 1 banana

Dinner:

- Lean Meat (poultry, beef, fish, etc.) 4 ounces
- Green Veggies 1 cup
- 1/3 avocado

Snack:

- Protein Shake
- Peanut Butter or Almond Butter 1 tablespoon

6 Biggest Diet Flaws

Some diet flaws can really bring our entire exercise and nutrition program down, so it's very important to be aware of them, so that we can avoid them at all costs!

Sugar

This is one of the biggest flaws in any diet. Many health problems derive from it, including diabetes. The safest thing you can do is cut it out completely.

Ultra-Low Calorie Diet

Eating almost nothing is a bad idea. For one thing, it slows your metabolism right down meaning that your fat loss is combined with muscle loss. Secondly, everyone returns to their dreadful eating habits eventually – this diet is unsustainable.

Highly-Processed Foods

Processed foods don't satiate you at all, and your body doesn't absorb them well. Nature intended that we should be eating raw food, or at the very least, minimally processed, and so that is what we should aim for.

Wrong Amount of Calories

The calories that we consume need to be less than the calories burned. Consume the wrong amount of calories for your goal, and you *will* fail. So having knowledge about the number of calories needed is vital.

For example, if your goal is to gain muscle, then add 200-500 calories per day. If your goal is to lose fat, then subtract 200-500 calories per day. It really is as simple as that.

Wrong Macronutrients

Protein is the best macronutrient of all, but you also need to eat carbohydrates and fats. Getting the ratios right is vital. The chart below gives a generalized example of the amount of each food group that we need to consume daily to stay healthy:

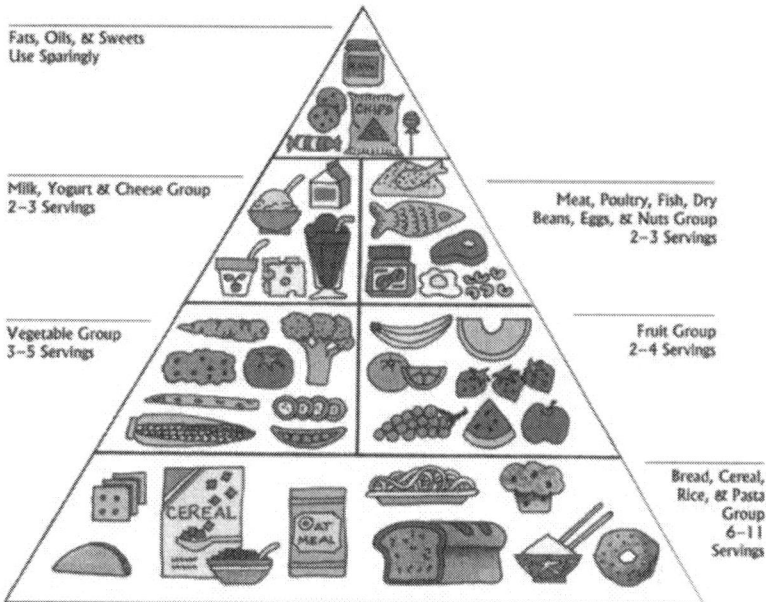

Relying on Supplements

Supplements were created to supplement your training and diet, not to replace them. Use them only for convenience.

Weight Management Tips

Gaining an overall better relationship with food is much more successful than yoyo dieting. Here is a **selection of tips** to help you with this:

- Avoid faddy diets. They leave you feeling deprived and are unhealthy. Any weight you lose won't stay off.
- Put a stop to emotional eating. Don't eat when you're bored, stressed or unhappy. Find other ways to distract yourself.
- Eat in a more mindful way. Mindfulness studies show that paying attention while you eat, instead of watching TV or looking at your phone, means that you eat the right amount.

- Fill up on fruit and vegetables instead of empty calories. The high water and fibre content in most fresh fruits and vegetables makes them tough to overeat. You'll feel full long before you've overdone it on the calories.

- Don't deny yourself anything. You can eat treats, but in moderation.

- Drink water to help you fill up. Making the healthy lifestyle change might be difficult to start with, but will soon become habit.

- Sleep well. Lack of sleep can have a very negative effect on your diet. Don't let that be your downfall!

- Train your brain. We aren't born with an inborn craving for French fries and donuts or an aversion to broccoli and whole grains. This conditioning happens over time as we're exposed to more and unhealthier food choices. You just need to spend some time retraining your mind.

- It's essential to remember that it isn't just about the *amount* of calories that you eat. Each type of food reacts with each individual differently, so pay attention to what your body is telling you.

- It takes time. This is the most important lesson. You won't lose weight all in one go, so don't give up, even when it doesn't seem like you'll ever reach your goal. Stick at it and you will.

5 Supplements To Consider

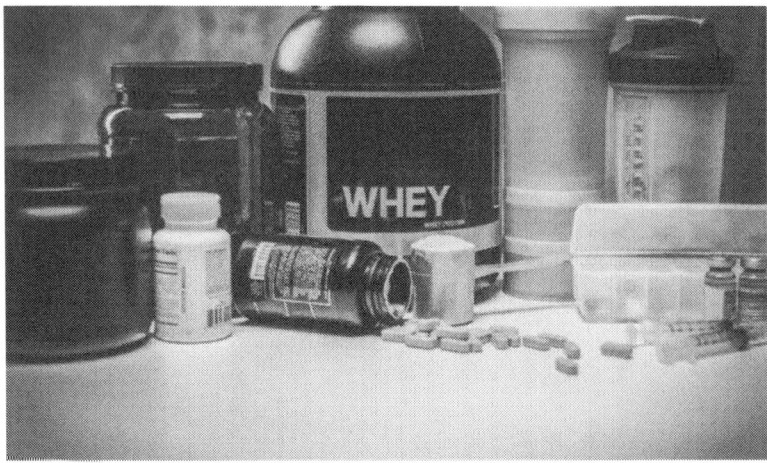

Many calisthenics athletes do not take supplements, but they are something you might like to consider. Here are the top 5 for you to think about.

Although supplements cannot replace proper nutrition, they can help you hit your fitness goals faster. Regardless of what your training goals are, the proper supplements can help improve your health, performance and physique.

Protein

Protein supplements work fast and allow you to easily and affordably meet your daily protein objectives, even when you're busy at work. Because whey protein is digested quickly and easily, it's the ideal after-workout protein source.

Fish Oil

Fish oil's numerous benefits come from its high levels of omega-3 fatty acids. Omega-3s are considered *essential fatty acids*. This implies they're essential for human health, but are not made by the body. Fish oil is an essential supplement, whether you're attempting to develop muscle, burn fat, or boost overall health.

Branched Chain Amino Acids

When consumed during training, BCAAs can advance prolonged performance and promote recovery. BCAAs may also reduce muscle breakdown (catabolism), potentially leading to more total muscle growth.

Glutamine

Glutamine is an adaptogenic amino acid in protein. It's the most plentiful amino acid in skeletal muscle, and also plays an important role in immune system health and the wellbeing of the whole body. In supplement form, glutamine can produce additional benefits to help build muscle mass.

Creatine

Creatine is one of the most-well-studied supplements on the market. It has been proven to improve sprint times and boost the performance of athletes involved in high-intensity activity, such as weightlifting and strength training.

10 SAFETY TIPS YOU SHOULD NEVER IGNORE

1. Always take 5 to 10 minutes to warm up and cool down properly.
2. Plan to start gradually and boost your activity level slowly unless you are already exercising regularly and vigorously.
3. Take note that training too hard or too often can cause overuse injuries like stress fractures, stiff or sore joints and muscles, and inflamed tendons and ligaments. Sports provoking repetitive wear and tear on certain parts of your body - like swimming (shoulders), jogging (knees, ankles, and feet), and tennis (elbows) - are frequently overuse culprits, too. A mix of different types of activities and adequate rest is safer.
4. Be attentive to your body. Keep off on exercise when you're sick or feeling very tired. Cut back if you cannot complete an exercise session, feel faint after exercise or tired during the day, or suffer persistent aches and pains in joints after exercising.
5. If you break exercising for a while, drop back to a lower level of exercise initially. If you're doing strength exercise, for example, do fewer reps or sets.
6. For many people, just drinking plenty of water is enough. But if you're working out particularly hard or doing a marathon or triathlon, pick drinks that replace fluids plus essential electrolytes.
7. Select clothes and shoes designed for your type of exercise. Replace shoes every six months as cushioning wears out.

8. For strength exercise, good form is vital. Initially use no weight, or very light additional weights, when learning the exercises. Don't sacrifice good form by hurrying to finish reps or sets, or struggling to use extra weights.

9. Training vigorously in hot, humid conditions can lead to severe overheating and dehydration. Reduce your pace when the temperature rises above 70°F. On days when the temperature is anticipated to reach 80°F, train during cooler morning or evening hours or at an air-conditioned location. Lookout for signs of overheating, like headache, dizziness, nausea, faintness, cramps, or palpitations.

10. Dress appropriately for cold-weather workouts to circumvent hypothermia. Depending on the temperature, wear layers you can peel off as you warm up. Don't forget gloves.

Delayed muscle soreness that arises 12 to 24 hours after a workout and gradually subsides is a normal response to taxing your muscles. By contrast, insistent or intense muscle pain that begins during a workout or right after, or muscle soreness that persists more than one to two weeks, deserves a call to your doctor for advice.

20 TIPS TRAINERS WISH YOU KNEW ABOUT YOUR WORKOUT

Here are some **interesting facts you didn't know** about exercising and your body.

- The human body consists of over 600 individual muscles.
- Astonishingly, if you get all your muscles working together, you can roughly lift close to 50,000 pounds!
- Frequent exercise can reduce the signs and symptoms of PMS.
- People who cross-train with a diversity of exercises, are overall more fit, healthy and less prone to injury.
- For every 25 pounds of excess weight, your body needs to pump blood through an extra 5,000 miles of blood vessels. If you're 100 pounds overweight that would be 500 000 miles.
- It takes 70 muscles for you to utter a single word.

To ensure that you reap all of the benefits from the exercise, **follow these top tips**.

1. Embrace reps
Don't be afraid to sets of high reps. If you want to build muscle, more reps is what you need.

2. Work Hard

You need to keep going no matter what. When you want to quit…don't! Keep your end goal in mind at all times. Push through the pain.

3. Use Simple, Compound Exercises

Stick to exercises that you can do, but that help you work your muscles. Simple doesn't necessarily mean easy. For example, focus on:

- Pull-ups
- Bodyweight Squats, pistols and shrimp squats
- Push-ups
- Australian Pull-up variations
- Dips
- Bridges
- Handstand push-ups (against a wall - lower skill, more effort)
- Leg raises

And progress from there.

4. Limit Sets

Calisthenics is all about high intensity in a short period of time. Don't ruin that by increasing the sets. It'll just have negative consequences.

5. Focus on Progress and Utilize a Training Journal

Keep a journal to ensure that you don't get stuck. Constant progress is key to calisthenics.

6. Have Plenty of Rest - You Grow When You Rest

Rest is vital. That's when your muscles grow, so don't forget it.

7. Quit Eating "Clean" the Whole Time!

Ensure that your diet is balanced. Moderation, not denial.

8. Sleep More

When you sleep:

- Your brain produces Growth Hormone.
- The brain produces natural melatonin – probably the most powerful healing immunity compound known to science.
- When you sleep, you brain produces Luteinizing Hormone, which powerfully stimulates the interstitial cells to produce testosterone – the number-one bodybuilding chemical powerhouse.

9. Train the Mind Along With the Body

Your mind-set is absolutely vital to keep yourself going. If you go into it with the wrong attitude, you're setting yourself up for failure.

10. Get Strong

If you desire to gain as much muscle as your genetic potential will allow, just exercising your muscles won't cut it. You need to train your nervous system too.

11. Be Consistent

Work constantly, stick to a routine and keep it up!

12. Follow an Effective Exercise Routine

Find out what exercises work for you, and incorporate them into your routine.

13. Set Realistic Goals

Having something to aim for, keeps you going. Just don't set unattainable goals or you wont stick at it.

14. Use the Buddy System

Having someone to workout alongside will keep you going much longer than if you're doing it alone.

15. Make Your Plan Fit Your Life

The great thing about calisthenics is that you can fit it in alongside a busy lifestyle. If you're dedicated enough, finding time for the short workouts won't be too difficult.

16. Be Happy

Enjoy what you're doing. Choosing exercises you like is essential to keeping going.

17. Watch the Clock

Watch your body clock and work out the time of day that you have most energy. Use that to your advantage.

18. Call In the Pros

If you're just getting started, having a professional help you can be very beneficial.

19. Get Inspired

Someone will inspire you. Use that to help you!

20. Be Patient

It won't happen overnight, but keeping going is vital to success.

19 COMMON MISTAKES THAT ARE KILLING YOUR RESULTS

1. Improper Grip

This has got to be one of the most hotly contested subjects within the Calisthenics & Street Workout Community. Which grip is proper and which is incorrect. We were taught to put thumb aligned on the same side with your fingers. But the proper grip is what ensures you the most possible leverage, and that means wrapping your thumb around the bar. There are obvious pros and cons to each, such as wrist grip strength, but wouldn't you want the most secure grip in anything you do?

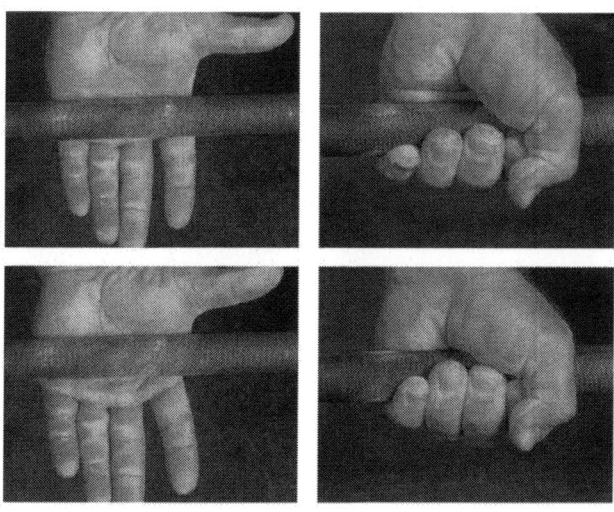

2. Squat Form

Deep squats are by far one of the staples of Calisthenics and good form is essential. ExRx.net has a guide for the proper form on deep squats.

3. Not Full Range of Motion Pull Ups or Other Exercise Movements

As utilized in the biomedical and weightlifting communities, range of motion refers to the distance and direction a joint can move between the flexed position and the extended position. The act of attempting to increase this distance through therapeutic exercises (range of motion therapy – stretching from flexion to extension for physiological gain) is also sometimes called range of motion. In other words full range of motion means fully extending.

Many people cut short literally their range of motion and as a result cut short their opportunities for growth.

4. Elbows Flare Out

This should never happen for exercises like dips or push ups.

5. Dips – Too Low or Not Too Low

6. Too Many Reps or Sets

Doing too many reps or set and not having enough rest will result in over training.

7. Neglect Legs

Some simply skip legs for their routine which results in body disproportion.

8. No Rest Days (Over training)

Doing too much, thinking more is better

9. Overdeveloped Anterior Deltoids

This happens because of Lats Pattern Overload

10. Kipping Muscle Ups Is Not Strict Muscle Up

11. Not Thinking About What You Are Doing

Always know what you are doing, have a plan and know how to improve your knowledge for each exercise you practice.

12. Comparing Yourself to Others

Your physiology and abilities are unique. Try to not look at others, instead strive to be better than you were yesterday.

13. Focusing on Strengths, Favourite Exercises and Body Parts

Never neglect your weakness and don't concentrate too much on your favourite exercises. Focus on the hardest exercise instead.

14. Not Completely Focusing on Workout

Try to avoid distractions by all means and have a total focus on your workout.

15. Setting Unrealistic Goals

16. Resting Too Much

Resting too much will make your body cool down which will increase a chance of injury.

17. Not Warming Up Properly

Make sure to always warm up for at least 5 to 10 minutes to get yourself ready for the heavy training.

18. Sticking to the Same Old Routine

Principle of Adaption states that your body adapts to the physical challenge and if you don't progress, your body won't make any stronger.

19. Quality versus Quantity

Put all of your effort to quality and never to quantity.

FAQ

1. Are calisthenics enough for weight training?

Yes, and this is because it improves your functional strength, as shown by Collective Evolution, as long as you find the best workout for yourself. Everyone has individual needs.

2. What is best, Calisthenics or Weight Lifting?

This is examined in details in the Calisthenics chapter of this book. There are pros and cons to each workout, and only you can decide which one suits your individual needs and lifestyle best.

3. Can calisthenics be used for strength, endurance and muscle building?

In short, yes. Depending on what workout you go for, calisthenics can be tailored to your personalized requirements.

For more information watch 'Calisthenics Exercises – Build Muscle, Strength, and Endurance'.

4. Do calisthenics build muscle mass?

You can use calisthenics purely to build muscle mass depending on the exercises you chose to do. The three most important exercises for building strength and muscle are push-ups, pull-ups and squats.

5. How do you build bulk muscle by doing calisthenics?

Building muscle with calisthenics is done by selecting the right workouts for you. This has been examined in detail in the Exercises chapter of this guide. The trick here is to constantly challenge yourself to increase reps so you can progress to harder exercise. Try to find variations that would cause you fatigue at around 10-15 reps and perform 3 or 4 sets of each exercise. Perform two of the following movements in your workout: pushing, pulling and squatting.

6. Can calisthenics help you build your stamina?

Calisthenics is brilliant at helping you build stamina and endurance. This is another sector that has more detail in the Exercises segment of the book. Livestrong also has a lot of information on the topic.

7. Can calisthenics get you ripped?

It is commonly believed that only weight lifting will get you ripped, but as demonstrated by this book, calisthenics can be just as effective.

8. What are the best forearm calisthenics exercises?

There are a wide number of great forearm calisthenics exercises, as looked at in the Exercises chapter of this book. Most of the upper body exercises involve forearms. There are also some additional exercises you can perform with some extra weights:

- Flex and stretch all fingers, while making a complete fist for 30 seconds. Next, open and close your fingers do 2 sets of each for a total of a minute.

- Flex your wrist and hold in maximum flex for 30 seconds with the elbow straight but not locked.

- Extend your wrist with the elbow straight for 30 seconds. Do 2 sets for a total of 2 minutes.

These first three stretching exercises will get you ready for the more complex and more intense weight-bearing exercises to improve muscular development and the strength of the forearm.

- ***Seated Wrist Hammer Curls*** - In a seated position with your back straight, put your forearm on your thighs with your thumbs pointed upward. Use a 5-, 10-, or 20lb weight in a hammer position and raise it back and forth gradually for 3 sets of 20 repetitions. This will mature your brachioradialis muscle, which inserts at the distal aspect of the forearm at the wrist. Better hypertrophy of this muscle will give more definition and balance of the forearm.

- ***Seated Wrist Straight Curls*** - This is to improve your flexor muscles. In a seated posture, with your forearms on your thighs and palms facing upward, with a 5-, 10-, or even 20lb weight in hand, flex your wrist upward. Keep the forearms well placed against your thighs for greater balance and isolation of the wrist and forearm musculature. Ensure to place the wrist three to four inches away from the knee to allow the full range of motion. Do 3 sets of 20 repetitions.

- **Seated Reverse Wrist Curls** - This is to improve your extensor muscles and is also performed in a seated position with your forearms on your thigh, palms facing downward, with the wrist three to four inches away from the knees. Grip the weight and fully extend the wrist. Do this for 3 sets of 20 and take note not to lift the elbows from the thighs when extending the wrists. Keep the palms down.

- **Finger Curls** - This is a simple workout to perform and will improve finger and hand strength. Simply sit and hold a 5-, 10-, or 15lb in weight your hand. Turn your hand with the palm upward with the back of your wrist on your thigh. Let the weight to roll down your fingers, and now curl your fingers back holding the weight safely. Remember to keep the back of your wrist against your thigh throughout the execution of the exercise. Use weight which you can efficiently control and execute the exercises properly.

9. What are some calisthenics exercises that can exercise every (or most) of your muscles?

Ab Machine Guide is a *great resource* of information for calisthenics exercises and what muscles they work out. A lot of the exercises are tailored to specific muscles, but you can use the Workouts in this guide to target your whole body.

10. Is calisthenics the greatest strength and endurance exercise?

Everyone is different, which means that everyone's results will be personalized to them. However, research shows that people have the most success in building strength and endurance by following a calisthenics workout program.

11. How long should I do calisthenics?

This depends on your end goal and the subsequent workout plan you choose. Some workout plans are merely for a few weeks, some are for six months. It can even be a lifestyle change and something that you keep up forever.

12. What's the difference between calisthenics and bodyweight exercises?

They are very similar, with varying degrees of difficulty.

Calisthenics are a form of exercise consisting of a variety of exercises, often rhythmical movements, generally without using equipment or apparatus, using only one's body weight for resistance.

Bodyweight exercises are strength training exercises that do not require free weights; the practitioner's own weight provides the resistance for the movement.

13. Why does the military use calisthenics more than using weights?

While weight lifting is a useful form of training - particularly for the military - it uses a lot of equipment, which can be logistically problematic. There are also fewer accidents associated with calisthenics. You can read more about this at the Military website.

14. How long should you rest between Calisthenics sets?

This is dependent on the workout program you are using, and the results you're aiming for. Rest is essential because that's when you grow and for beginners 3 days a week rest is recommended. The chapter with the Workouts in this book will give you an idea about rest.

15. Is it ok to do calisthenics or bodyweight exercises daily?

Your recovery time is extremely important to your workout and must not be ignored or forgotten about. If you intend to do it daily, you should split your workout time between these days, as described in the Getting_Started chapter of this book.

16. Can doing intense calisthenics 3 days a week be a formidable workout?

Combined with the right diet and lifestyle, 3 days a week can certainly be sufficient as a workout, particularly for beginners. Any less isn't recommended.

17. How many sets and reps of bodyweight exercises is best for building muscle and strength?

This is dependent on your skill level. The Workout chapter of this book covers a beginner muscle building plan which gives details for this. You just need to ensure that you push yourself to your limit.

18. What workouts should I do to gain muscle using bodyweight?

The Exercises chapter of this book will give you a selection of workouts to get you started. You will need to do full body Workouts to ensure all of your muscles are targeted.

19. What kind of exercise is recommended to lose weight without equipment?

There are a whole range of exercises you can do at home to help you lose weight, as shown by the weight loss workout program in the Training chapter of this book.

20. How can I get stronger with bodyweight exercises?

Getting stronger with bodyweight exercises is all about picking the right workout for you. Take a look at the intermediate or advanced exercises, which will definitely help you gain strength.

CONCLUSION

So now that you've seen exactly *why* you should get started and *how* to begin, you'll have no issues in turning your life around! This book has covered everything you'll need to know including exercises, workout plans and top tips.

Here are the **benefits of calisthenics**, just as a reminder:

1. Exercise at home with no equipment

The most apparent benefit of calisthenics is that you virtually don't need any equipment or a lot of space to work out. In other words, you don't have to leave home. And this brings other profits: in terms of time efficacy, this implies you don't have to spend time to travel to the gym, and then back home; in monetary terms, you don't have to pay for the gym membership.

Performing calisthenics, you can (but you don't have to) use a pull-up bar, a jumping rope, or a resistance band or TRX, which are very cheap and may be easily installed in your house.

2. Strengthen the whole body

Many calisthenics exercises involve more than one muscle group. Take a typical push-ups, for example: you essentially work your chest (or the triceps, depending on the push-up's variation); yet to do a good push-up you have to brace the whole body as well as the quads, the gluteus, the core and abs. What is more, these muscles have to work in concord and tone in the right moment – which brings us to the next advantage of calisthenics – co-ordination.

3. Develop coordination

It's not just strength that you improve doing calisthenics, but it's also coordination. Without the collaboration of various body parts, the correct order and rhythm of movements, you wouldn't be able to do a single rep of burpees, jump rope, or pull up on the bar. Performing calisthenics, you increase your body's motoricity as a whole – mind you that strength is not the only component of fitness.

4. Develop flexibility

Another characteristic of physical capability which can be established thanks to calisthenics is flexibility. Most of body-weight workouts include an extended movement amplitude – the movements are wholly extended – which results in building strength without loss in flexibility. That doesn't imply, however, that you don't have to stretch if you do crunches, lunges, or squats.

You should do some dynamic stretching at the end of your warm-up, and static stretching at the end of your exercise session. This works in a kind of a circle – the more flexible you are, the broader the range of movements in your workout – and thus the greater the effectiveness of exercises. The wider the range of movements in the exercises, the better for your flexibility.

5. Develop endurance

Lastly, if the calisthenics exercises are properly done in the adjusted number of reps and sets, they can really boost your body's endurance. Especially great for the muscles' endurance are body-weight exercises which require holding still a position for some amount of time. Great examples are plank (in different variations) or v-sit.

6. Lose fat effectively

If your objective is burning fat, calisthenics should be your best friend. But for cardio, your workout should also include some strength exercises to build muscles and lose weight more efficiently shaping up your figure at the same time. The calisthenics can be carefully done with high intensity, and that's why they are really great for fat fighters. Make sure you look up HIIT and Tabata workout to find out some more about harmless and effective ways for weight loss.

7. Avoid monotony

HIIT and Tabata regimens are only two ways for establishing your calisthenic exercises. You may also attempt circuits or pyramids to do calisthenics with the best effectiveness and time efficiency. If you do work out on the gym with loads, you may also accompaniment your workout plan with some calisthenics – just to do something diverse from time to time. The more diversity in your workout, the greater the encouragement to keep going.

ABOUT THE AUTHOR

John Cooper was born in the United States, but as an army brat, spent most of his childhood traveling the world with his family. It was his own service in the military that first sparked his interest in fitness and, eventually in calisthenics. His drive to learn as much as he could about this type of bodyweight exercises led him to training his fellow soldiers.

After being discharged from the military, Cooper became a personal trainer. He began working with clients to help them lose weight, build muscle, and achieve their goals. It was during this time that he really began to develop his own training programs - for beginners, intermediates, and for experts.

These programs became the foundation for his book. Over his years of military service and working with clients, he has learned everything there is to know about calisthenics and has found the most effective and most valuable workouts for those at every level and for both men and women, no matter what their fitness goals are. His program and philosophy have left clients fitter than they have ever been before, and now Cooper is bringing that knowledge to the world!

Printed in Great Britain
by Amazon